3-D HUMAN BODY

LONDON, NEW YORK, MELBOURNE, MUNICH, AND DELHI

Senior Editor Carron Brown
Project Editor Steven Carton
Senior Art Editor Smiljka Surla
Designer Daniela Boraschi

Managing Editor Linda Esposito
Managing Art Editor Jim Green

Category Publisher Laura Buller
Design Development Manager Sophia M. Tampakopoulos

Senior Production Controller Angela Graef
Production Editor Andy Hilliard
DK Picture Library Claire Bowers
Picture Researcher Martin Copeland
Jacket Editor Matilda Gollon
Jacket Designer Yumiko Tahata
U.S. Editor John Searcy

3-D Digital Artist Arran Lewis

For Digital Labs International:
Director Maurice Linscott
Director of Animation Rob Cook
Programmer Steve Clare

AUGMENTED BY
TOTAL IMMERSION

First American Edition, 2011

Published in the United States by
DK Publishing
375 Hudson Street
New York, New York 10014

11 12 13 14 15 10 9 8 7 6 5 4 3 2 1
001—179064—Jan/2011

A catalog record for this book is available
from the Library of Congress.

ISBN 978-0-7566-7216-4

Hi-res workflow proofed by MDP, UK
Printed and bound in China by Toppan

**See our complete catalogue at
www.dk.com**

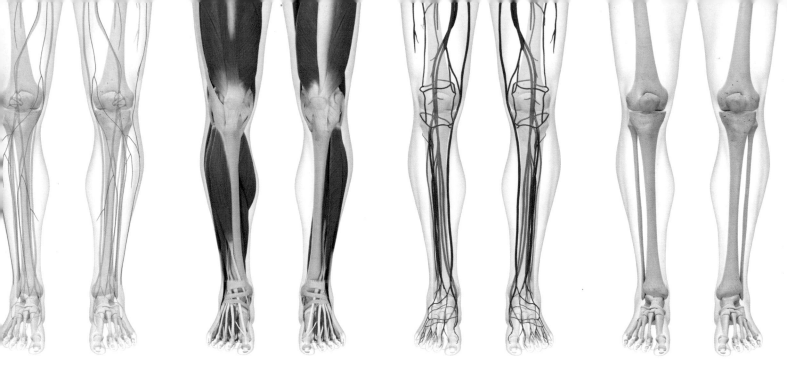

3-D HUMAN BODY

written by
Richard Walker

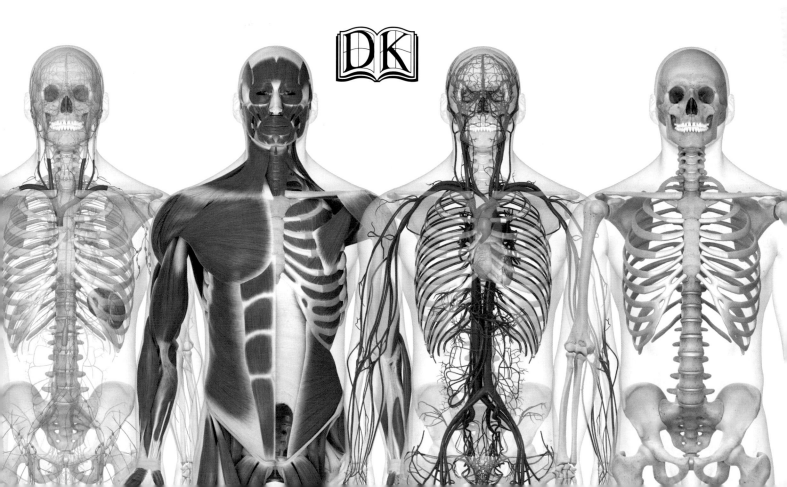

Contents

VIEW THE ANIMATIONS

1 Download the software from www.3Dpops.dkonline.com and follow the on-screen instructions to install the software on your computer.

2 In the book there are six Augmented Reality (AR) spreads. Look for the blue logo in the top right-hand corner of a page.

3 Sit at the computer with the book in front of you and your webcam turned on, and make sure that your book is in view of the webcam.

Show the main image to your webcam to start the AR animation.

Place your hand over each trigger box to control the human body's actions.

Beating he

The power plant of the circulatory system, the heart is a muscular pu that pushes blood around the boc supply every cell with food and ox Made of cardiac muscle, which co spontaneously and without tiring, heart beats around 2.5 billion times average lifetime without taking a b

OUTSIDE VIEW

1 Around the size of fis clenched fist, the heart is located in the chest between the two lungs. Visible from the outside are the muscular wall of the heart that contracts to pump blood, the coronary arteries, and the heart's major blood vessels.

HOW THE HEART BEATS

2 Relaxed heart
Each heartbeat cycle has three pacemaker. Initially, the atria and (pacemaker. Initially, the atria and ventricles relax, and blood from flows into the right and left...

Atria contract
The right and left atria then contract, squeezing blood through open valves into the ventricles, fill the two lower chambers of the heart pump blood.

STOPPING BACKFLOW
During each heartbeat cycle, valves in the heart prevent blood from flowing in the wrong direction. These semilunar valves, which guard the exits from the right and left ventricles, open to let blood out of the heart when the ventricles contract, but close when the ventricles relax.

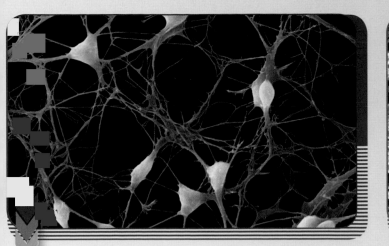

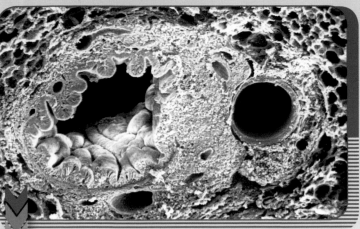

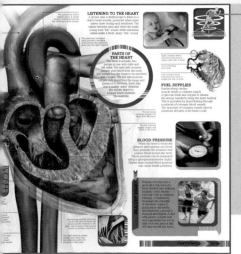

The AR logo is in the right-hand corner of the AR spread.

4 Show the central image on the open page to the webcam and the AR animation will jump to life from the pages of your book and appear on your computer screen.

5 To see the next part of the animation and make the human body do different things, place your hand over one of the trigger boxes. Each trigger box is labeled with a hand symbol to show that it is a trigger box, and the boxes are numbered in the order that they should be covered.

Minimum system requirements

Windows PC
Windows XP with DirectX 9.0c (or Windows XP SP2), Windows Vista
Intel P4 2.4 GHz or Amd equivalent
1 Gb RAM
Supports most graphics cards (Nvidia, ATI, Chipset Intel) except Via chipset

Macintosh
Mac OS 10.4, 10.5, 10.6
Intel Dual Core (or Core 2 duo) 2.4Ghz
1 Gb RAM
Supports graphics cards Nvidia, ATI
(Macs based on Power PC processor are not supported)

Basics

Ovum (human egg cell) in fallopian tube

All of us started life as a single cell that contained a master set of instructions, inherited from our mother and father, for building a human body. As that cell multiplied, those instructions shaped and organized its trillions of offspring into the tissues and organs that form a recognizable human being. It produced the bones and muscles that support and move the body, the skin that covers it, and, of course, the means to produce new life.

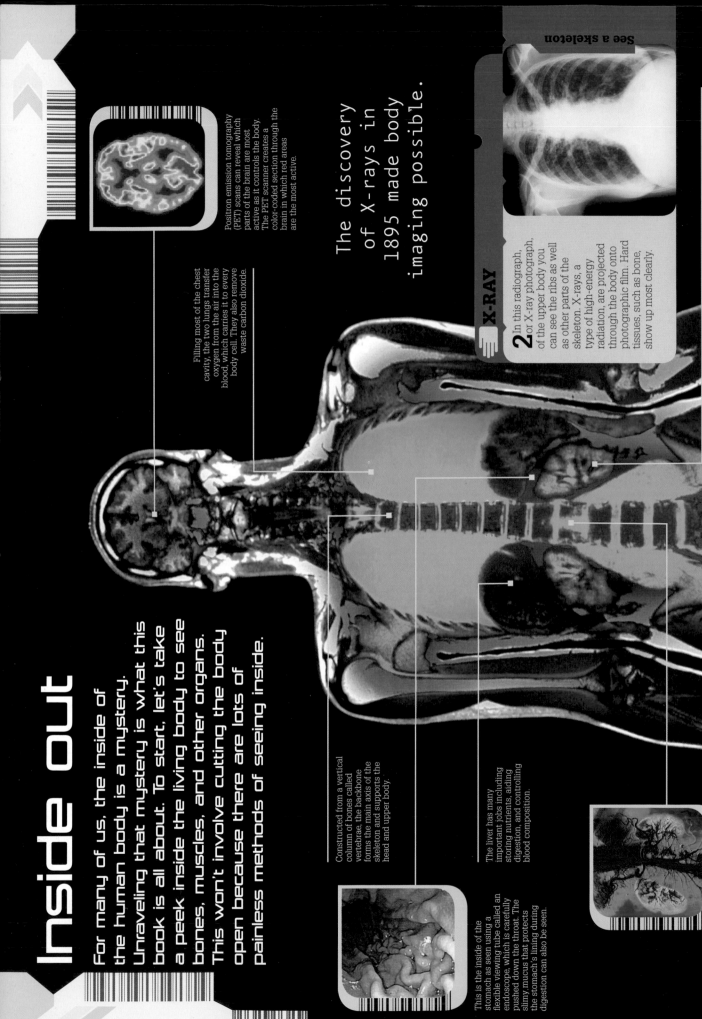

Inside out

For many of us, the inside of the human body is a mystery. Unraveling that mystery is what this book is all about. To start, let's take a peek inside the living body to see bones, muscles, and other organs. This won't involve cutting the body open because there are lots of painless methods of seeing inside.

The discovery of X-rays in 1895 made body imaging possible.

Positron emission tomography (PET) scans can reveal which parts of the brain are most active as it controls the body. The PET scanner creates a color-coded section through the brain in which red areas are the most active.

Filling most of the chest cavity, the two lungs transfer oxygen from the air into the blood, which carries it to every body cell. They also remove waste carbon dioxide.

X-RAY

2 In this radiograph, or X-ray photograph, of the upper body you can see the ribs as well as other parts of the skeleton. X-rays, a type of high-energy radiation, are projected through the body onto photographic film. Hard tissues, such as bone, show up most clearly.

The two kidneys remove waste and excess water from the blood that flows through them. Together, the waste and water form urine, which is released from the body.

Constructed from a vertical column of bones called vertebrae, the backbone forms the main axis of the skeleton and supports the head and upper body.

The liver has many important jobs including storing nutrients, aiding digestion, and controlling blood composition.

This is the inside of the stomach as seen using a flexible viewing tube called an endoscope, which is carefully pushed down the throat. The slimy mucus that protects the stomach's lining during digestion can also be seen.

Blood vessels (red) supplying the kidneys (yellow) are seen in this angiogram, a type of X-ray. The image is made by injecting a substance into blood that is opaque to X-rays so the blood vessels stand out.

To make this radionuclide scan, a radioactive substance is injected into the bloodstream and taken up by the bones. They give off rays that turn into an image indicating cell activity.

The fleshy front of the thigh is shaped by the quadriceps femoris, a big muscle group that pulls the lower leg to straighten the knee.

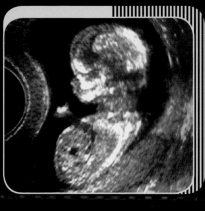

ULTRASOUND

This image of a fetus inside its mother was produced using ultrasound scanning. High-frequency sound waves (ultrasounds) are beamed into the body and bounce off tissues and organs, creating echoes that are analyzed by a computer to create a picture.

Each foot is made of 26 bones that together form a sturdy platform that bends at the ankle. The feet support the body and push it off the ground during walking.

The body's biggest bone, the femur (thighbone), connects the hip bone (into which its rounded end fits) to the knee, and supports the body's weight.

The knee joint, between the femur and tibia (shin bone), is the body's biggest. Joints between bones allow them to move and give the skeleton its flexibility.

CT SCAN

Lungs surround heart (top center)

Skeletal muscle covers the skeleton

View the muscles

1 Computed tomography (CT) scanning uses a computer to analyze X-rays beamed through a person to create images in the form of body "slices," such as this one through the chest. CT scans reveal both hard tissues, such as bone (yellow), and soft tissues, such as skeletal muscle.

THE BODY

This remarkable picture of the body's interior was produced using magnetic resonance imaging (MRI). MRI is just one of many techniques that allow us to see inside a living body. Others include endoscopy, CT scans, PET scans, radionuclide scans, X-rays, and ultrasound. MRI scans use powerful magnets and radio waves to produce a detailed image of organs and tissues. This section through a person shows some key organs, such as the lungs, liver, and kidneys.

Organization

Your body is built from trillions of microscopic living units called cells. They come in many shapes, sizes, and appearances, related to the specific job each performs. Cells are organized into tissues, of which there are four basic types—epithelial, connective, muscle, and nervous. Different types of tissues work together to construct organs and the body itself.

Cytoplasm, found between the cell membrane and the nucleus, consists of a transparent, jellylike fluid and the organelles that are suspended and move in it.

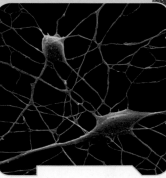

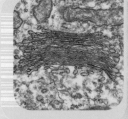

A Golgi complex (shown here in cross section) is a stack of flattened membrane bags that processes and packages proteins received from the rough endoplasmic reticulum so they are ready for export from, or use inside, the cell.

ZOOMING IN

Individual cells are tiny and invisible to the naked eye. A light microscope reveals basic cell structures such as the cytoplasm and nucleus. However, it takes the much greater magnifying power of an electron microscope, such as this one, to zoom in on the organelles you can see here on screen.

Microvilli are tiny, fingerlike projections of the cell membrane in certain cells, such as those lining the small intestine. They increase the cell's surface area and thus help make the absorption of substances more efficient.

ALL SHAPES AND SIZES

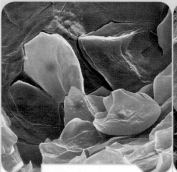

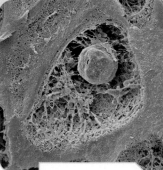

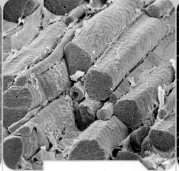

Epithelial tissue
Protective sheets of tightly packed cells, such as these from the tongue, cover the body and line hollow organs such as the mouth to prevent invasion by bacteria.

Connective tissue
Tissue such as cartilage (above), bone, and tendons forms a frame that supports and holds the body. It typically consists of cells (orange) within a matrix (gray).

Muscle tissue
This tissue is made from cells that get shorter to generate movement. Skeletal muscle (above) pulls bones to move them. Other types make the heart beat and move food.

Nervous tissue
The nervous system, the body's control and coordination network, is made from nervous tissue. Nerve cells transmit electrical signals via nerves, the spinal cord, and brain.

The cytoskeleton is the network of fine rods—microfilaments and microtubules—that forms a framework that supports cell structures, shapes the cell, and also moves organelles through the cytoplasm.

A lysosome is a membrane bag filled with powerful digestive enzymes that break down worn-out organelles.

BUILDING A BODY

Cells of the same type are organized into tissues. Two or more tissues together make an organ, such as the lung. Organs that work together make up one of the 12 systems that interact to make a living body. Here, epithelial tissue (pink) and connective tissue (brown), with other tissues, form the trachea, an organ that is part of the respiratory (breathing) system.

Ribosomes are small, granular structures that make proteins, and build and run the cell using instructions received from the nucleus.

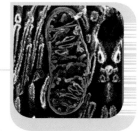

Mitochondria (one is called a mitochondrion; shown here in cross section) are the cell's power plants. They use oxygen to release energy for cell activities from glucose, in a process called cellular respiration.

The nucleus is the cell's control center. It houses genetic instructions, in the form of DNA, that are needed to build, maintain, and operate the cell.

INSIDE A CELL

Although cells are tiny (40 placed in a row would stretch across a period), they have a complex structure. As this typical body cell shows, each cell is bounded by a cell membrane, has a controlling nucleus, and is filled mainly with cytoplasm. The cytoplasm contains a highly organized array of structures called organelles. These perform a variety of jobs, including releasing energy and making proteins that keep the cell alive.

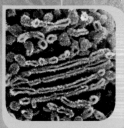

Rough endoplasmic reticulum, shown here in cross section, is a network of folded membranes that extends throughout the cell. It stores and transports various substances, including the proteins made in the ribosomes on its surface.

Around five million cells (including two million red blood cells) die and are replaced every second.

Building instructions

Every cell in our body contains the instructions needed to build and run that cell. These instructions, called genes, are inherited from our parents. Genes are contained in 46 chromosomes located in the nucleus of each cell. When cells divide, for growth or repair, their chromosomes are copied accurately so that each offspring cell has exactly the same genes.

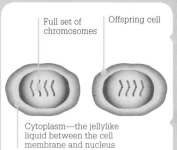

Chromosomes are normally long and thin. However, when a cell divides, its chromosomes shorten, thicken, and then duplicate themselves so they appear X-shaped.

This chromosome has been unraveled to show how it is constructed from coils of DNA that are curled upon themselves to form a supercoil.

The DNA double helix is organized into coils and supercoils that enable incredible lengths of DNA to be crammed into the tiny nucleus. In all, some 6.6 ft (2 m) of DNA is packed into a cell's 46 chromosomes.

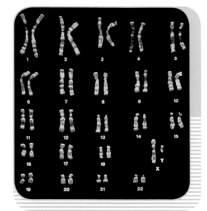

CHROMOSOMES

This photograph shows the two sets of 23 chromosomes in a nucleus, one set inherited from the mother and one from the father. The paired chromosomes have been arranged in order of size from 1 to 22. The 23rd pair are the sex chromosomes—XY in males (as here) and XX in females.

INSIDE THE NUCLEUS

Each chromosome inside the nucleus is made from a long molecule called DNA (deoxyribonucleic acid). Sections of DNA called genes contain the recipes for making proteins, which are used as enzymes to control chemical reactions, as building materials, as chemical messengers called hormones, and in many other roles. By controlling the production of proteins, DNA controls the cell.

Loops and twists enclose proteins associated with DNA, such as the histone shown here. Histone helps organize and package DNA, and also helps determine which genes are active in which types of body cells.

CELL DIVISION

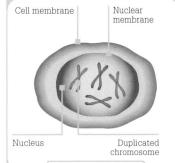 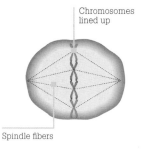 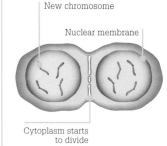

Cell membrane | Nuclear membrane

Chromosomes lined up

New chromosome

Nuclear membrane

Full set of chromosomes | Offspring cell

Nucleus | Duplicated chromosome

Spindle fibers

Cytoplasm starts to divide

Cytoplasm—the jellylike liquid between the cell membrane and nucleus

Preparation
Before cell division, or mitosis, begins, each chromosome duplicates itself so that it consists of two identical strands. To make things clearer, just four of the 46 chromosomes are shown here.

Lining up
As the nuclear membrane surrounding the chromosomes breaks down, a framework of thin fibers called the spindle forms. The duplicated chromosomes line up across the center of the spindle.

Separation
The chromosomes split and their strands are pulled to opposite ends of the cell by the spindle, which then disappears. A nuclear membrane forms around each group of new chromosomes.

Offspring
The "parent" cell's cytoplasm divides to form two offspring cells. These cells are exact copies of each other, their nuclei containing the same number of chromosomes, and identical genes.

Identical twins, such as these two girls, look the same because they share identical genes. However, their personalities will probably differ because of differences in life experiences.

SLIGHTLY DIFFERENT

Despite outward appearances, we are very alike in terms of DNA. One person's DNA is 99.9 percent the same as someone else's. That similarity reaches 99.95 percent between family members, and 100 percent in identical twins. However, small differences in DNA are enough, combined with the effects of our surroundings and upbringing, to make all of us individuals.

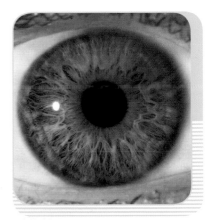

INHERITED GENES

The genes we inherit from our parents control our body's features, such as eye color. Like many other genes, eye-color genes have different versions, or alleles, each producing a variation of that feature. This explains why children may have blue, brown, or green eyes. The color of a child's eyes depends on which allele is inherited from the mother and which is from the father.

This protein (pepsin) is made from a sequence of amino-acid building blocks. A section of DNA— a gene—contains the instructions to put together amino acids in the right order to build the protein.

The bases (colored green, blue, red, and yellow) in DNA form the "letters" of the instructions, within each gene, that make a particular protein. Reading along the DNA strand, the sequence of bases determines the sequence of amino acids that makes the protein.

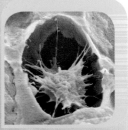

This bone cell (yellow) does not look the same as a brain cell, even though both contain the same DNA and genes. That's because certain genes are switched on or off in different cell types.

DNA is like a twisted ladder—the "uprights" (pink) are sugar and phosphate molecules, and the "rungs" are bases.

Replacements

Reproduction creates offspring to replace us when we die. Our reproductive systems are the only body systems that differ between males and females. Both make sex cells—sperm (male) and eggs (female)—and enable those cells to meet, following an intimate act called sexual intercourse, so that a new life is formed.

JOINING TOGETHER

If sperm that have survived the journey from the vagina meet an egg within 24 hours of its release in the fallopian tube, then fertilization occurs. Sperm (blue) surround the egg until one penetrates its outer layer. Fertilization occurs when this sperm's head fuses with the egg's nucleus (center).

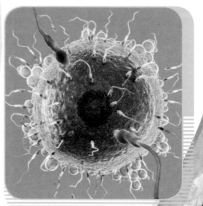

The seminal vesicles and prostate gland release fluids that mix with sperm to make a transport liquid called semen. They also activate sperm and provide them with energy.

The vas deferens is the tube that carries mature sperm from the epididymis to the urethra, which runs along the penis.

The bladder is part of the urinary system. It stores urine made in the kidneys before releasing it through the urethra.

MALE AND FEMALE

The male system consists of a pair of testes (which produce sperm), the penis, and the tubes that connect them. The female system consists of the two ovaries (which release eggs), two fallopian tubes, the uterus, and the vagina. During sexual intercourse, the penis introduces sperm into the vagina. If sperm and an egg meet, and fertilization occurs, the resulting baby develops inside the female's uterus until it is ready to be born.

The urethra is the tube that carries both sperm and urine outside the body.

The epididymis is a long, coiled tube where sperm that were produced in the testis mature.

The rectum is the last section of the large intestine, part of the digestive system.

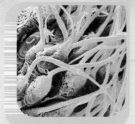

Sperm, seen here in production in the testis, have a head (orange) that contains genetic material (chromosomes) and a tail (blue) that enables them to swim.

The testis contains hundreds of tightly looped seminiferous tubules that produce millions of sperm daily.

The penis delivers millions of sperm into the female's vagina during sexual intercourse.

A man's testes produce 250 million sperm each day— that's around 3,000 per second.

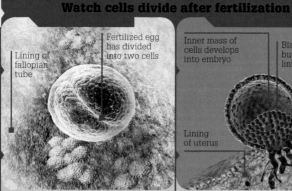

Lining of fallopian tube

Fertilized egg has divided into two cells

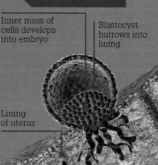

Inner mass of cells develops into embryo

Blastocyst burrows into lining

Lining of uterus

1 About 36 hours after fertilization, as it travels toward the uterus, the fertilized egg—containing chromosomes from both sperm and egg—divides into two identical cells. Cells then divide every 12 hours to produce 4, 8, 16, then 32 cells and, eventually, a hollow ball of cells called a blastocyst.

Six days after fertilization, the blastocyst reaches the uterus and burrows into its soft lining. Its inner cells divide and develop into an embryo that within a few weeks has organs such as the heart and liver. The blastocyst's outer cells form the placenta through which the embryo receives food and oxygen.

On average, pregnancy lasts 38 weeks from fertilization.

SEEING INSIDE

2 Two months after fertilization, the embryo is called a fetus. It is recognizably human with arms, legs, head, and trunk. Growth of the fetus inside its mother's uterus is checked using ultrasound scanning. This 3-D ultrasound scan shows the face of a 30-week-old fetus.

View the fetus

The fallopian tube carries a newly released egg from the ovary towards the uterus. It is also the site of fertilization.

The ovary contains thousands of immature eggs and releases one ripe (mature) egg each month in an adult woman.

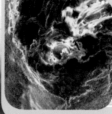

An egg bursts from the surface of an ovary during ovulation. This is part of the menstrual cycle—the sequence of events that occurs each month to prepare the uterus for possible pregnancy.

CHILD TO ADULT
After birth, we all go through the same processes of physical and mental development. In the teen years, rapid growth occurs, the body changes shape, and the reproductive system is switched on. This sequence of changes, called puberty, changes a child into an adult.

The uterus, or womb, is a hollow organ with a muscular wall that protects and nourishes a growing fetus during pregnancy.

The bladder is part of the urinary system. As in the male, it stores and releases urine.

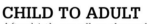

The urethra carries urine outside the body from the bladder.

The vagina links the uterus to the outside of the body and is the passageway for a baby during birth.

20 years old

The cervix is the neck of the uterus. It protrudes into, and connects to, the vagina.

13 years old

3 years old

1 year old

GROWING BONES
This sequence of X-rays of the hand illustrates how a part of the body, the skeleton, develops during the first 20 years of life. Some of the infant's skeleton is made of flexible cartilage, but this is replaced by bone tissue (purple) as the hand bones grow.

DEVELOPMENT

Skin deep

Our body's largest organ, skin provides us with a protective overcoat that is waterproof and self-repairing, and which stops pathogens (germs) from invading the body. It also protects us from harmful rays in sunlight, detects touch, and helps keep our body temperature constant. Hairs and nails grow from the skin to provide extra protection.

Hair shafts, rods made of dead cells filled with keratin, project above the skin's surface from hair follicles.

The epidermis is the upper part of the skin. It consists of several layers. The lowest layer contains actively dividing cells.

STEADY TEMPERATURE

The skin plays a key role in keeping the body's internal temperature at a steady 98.6°F (37°C). When it's hot, sweat glands release sweat that evaporates from the skin's surface (below) to cool the body, and blood vessels in the dermis widen to lose extra heat. In cold conditions, blood vessels narrow to minimize heat loss.

The dermis is the lower, more complex layer of the skin. It contains blood vessels, sensory receptors, and sweat glands.

Skin flakes (flat, dead epidermal cells) are removed from the surface of the skin with daily wear and tear. Around 50,000 skin flakes are lost from the skin's surface every minute.

Sweat glands produce watery sweat that travels along sweat ducts through the dermis and epidermis and onto the skin's surface.

GETTING A GRIP

The undersides of the fingertips are covered with swirling epidermal ridges that, like the tread of a running shoe, provide extra grip. On hard surfaces, these ridges leave behind sweaty patterns called fingerprints that are unique to each of us. For that reason, they are used by the police to identify criminals.

Sebaceous glands release oily sebum into hair follicles and onto the skin. Sebum lubricates and softens hairs and skin and makes them waterproof.

A hair follicle is a deep, narrow cavity in the skin in which the root of a hair is buried and from which a hair grows.

Skin is the body's heaviest organ, weighing about 11 lb (5 kg) in an adult.

SKIN LAYERS

Although just millimeters thick, skin has two layers—the upper epidermis and the lower dermis. The epidermis consists largely of dead, flattened cells, filled with tough, waterproof keratin, that protect the underlying dermis. As dead cells are worn away from the skin's surface, they are replaced by constantly dividing, living cells in the deep epidermis. The thicker dermis is more complex and contains various structures.

GROWING HAIR

There are around 100,000 thick, terminal hairs on the scalp, of which about 120 are lost daily. Having completed their growth, they are pushed out by new hairs. To form a new hair, cells at the base of the follicle divide and, as they are pushed upward, fill with keratin and die.

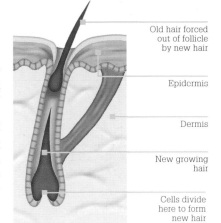

Old hair forced out of follicle by new hair

Epidermis

Dermis

New growing hair

Cells divide here to form new hair

The skin of older people is often wrinkled because their dermis produces far fewer of the collagen and elastin fibers that keep the skin of younger people firm, elastic, and wrinkle-free.

Dermal papillae are the pimplelike extensions of the dermis that prevent the epidermis and the dermis from separating.

Arteries supply oxygen and nutrients to skin cells and help control body temperature.

SKIN LIFE

Most people have tiny, sausage-shaped eyelash mites (below) living in the follicles of their eyelashes, where they feed on sebum and dead skin cells. Other occupants of the skin's surface include billions of bacteria. Most are harmless, but some can infect cuts in the skin's surface.

PIMPLE POWER

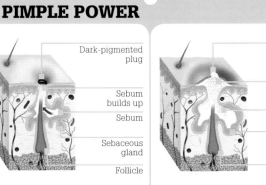

Dark-pigmented plug

Sebum builds up

Sebum

Sebaceous gland

Follicle

Plug

Bacteria builds up

Sebum

Sebaceous gland

Follicle

Blackhead
Acne (or pimples) is caused by blocked follicles and too much sebum. This can form a dark plug or blackhead that traps sebum inside the follicle.

Infected follicle
If skin bacteria infect the trapped sebum, the follicle becomes red and painful. When defensive white cells arrive to engulf the invading bacteria, they form creamy pus.

Subcutaneous fat layer under the dermis helps insulate the body and stores energy.

Nerve fibers carry signals to the brain from different types of sensory receptors, which detect touch, pressure, vibration, pain, or heat and cold.

Sensory receptor

Supporting framework

Making up around 20 percent of your weight, the skeleton is the framework of bones that supports and shapes your body, protects internal organs, and, being flexible, allows your body to move. Bones also make blood cells and store fat and calcium, which is essential for healthy teeth, nerves, and muscles.

The skull is a bony case that protects the brain and sense organs, forms the mouth, and shapes the face.

The clavicle (collarbone) extends from the sternum to the scapula, with which it forms the pectoral (shoulder) girdle that connects the arm to the axial skeleton.

The scapula (shoulder blade) is a flat, triangular bone with a hollow into which the rounded head of the humerus fits.

The ribs curve forward from the backbone toward the sternum, forming the rib cage that protects the chest organs and plays a key role in breathing.

The backbone (spine) is a strong, flexible chain of bones that holds the head and upper body upright. It is positioned directly over the legs and feet.

The pelvic (hip) girdle attaches the legs to the axial skeleton through the hip joints. It supports the organs of the abdomen.

The fibula is the smaller lower leg bone. It carries little body weight and, with the tibia, forms part of the ankle at its lower end.

Occipital bone

Parietal bone

Parietal bone

Temporal bone

Temporal bone

Zygomatic bone

Frontal bone

Zygomatic bone

Lacrimal bone

Lacrimal bone

Sphenoid bone

Vomer

Palatine bone

Palatine bone

Ethmoid bone

Inferior nasal concha

Inferior nasal concha

Nasal bones

Maxilla

Maxilla

Mandible

BRAIN CASE

The skull is constructed from 22 bones, 21 of which are locked together. Only the mandible (lower jaw) moves up and down so we can breathe, eat, and speak. Eight bones form the domed cranium that surrounds and protects the brain. The remaining bones shape the face.

There are 206 bones in the skeleton.

SKELETAL SYSTEM

An easy way to see how the skeletal system is put together is to divide it into the axial skeleton (white) and the appendicular skeleton (blue). The axial skeleton forms the main axis of the body and consists of the skull, backbone, ribs, and sternum. The appendicular skeleton, which is made up of 126 bones, includes the arms and legs, and the shoulder and hip girdles that attach them to the axial skeleton.

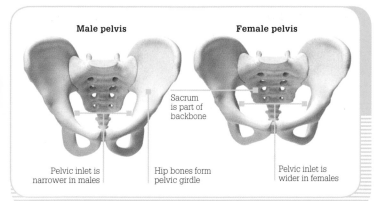

Male pelvis

Female pelvis

Sacrum is part of backbone

Pelvic inlet is narrower in males

Hip bones form pelvic girdle

Pelvic inlet is wider in females

MALE OR FEMALE?

Together, the sacrum and the pelvic girdle form the pelvis, the bowl-shaped structure that supports abdominal organs. Male and female pelvises differ. The pelvic inlet, the opening in the center of the pelvis, is broader in females to allow a baby's head to squeeze through during birth.

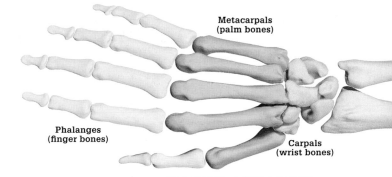

Metacarpals (palm bones)

Phalanges (finger bones)

Carpals (wrist bones)

HANDS AND FEET

Our hands and feet contain over half of the body's bones. Each is made of three types of bones, as shown here. Hands are very flexible and perform many tasks. Feet are much less flexible, but play a vital role in supporting and moving the body.

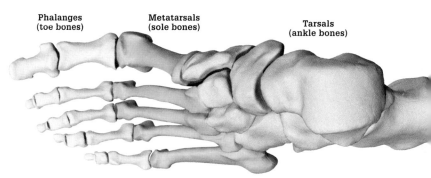

Phalanges (toe bones)

Metatarsals (sole bones)

Tarsals (ankle bones)

The humerus (upper arm bone) has a rounded head that fits into a socket in the scapula to form the shoulder joint.

The ulna is the inner bone of the forearm. The ulna and radius form the elbow joint where they meet the humerus.

There are 12 pairs of ribs, 10 of which are attached to the sternum by flexible cartilage (blue).

The lungs and heart (right) are key organs that the rib cage protects.

The sternum (breastbone) forms a bony, dagger-shaped shield at the front of the chest.

ORGAN PROTECTOR

The rib cage surrounds and protects the heart, lungs, and major blood vessels in the chest, as well as the liver and stomach in the abdomen. The 12 pairs of ribs curve forward around the chest wall from the backbone to meet up with the sternum.

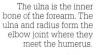

>> **CARTILAGE**

In addition to bone, the skeleton contains a tough, flexible tissue called cartilage. Cartilage shapes the ear pinna (outer flap), most of the nose, and the larynx (voice box). It also connects the ribs to the sternum and covers the ends of bones where they meet in joints.

The radius is the outer bone of the forearm. It runs from the elbow to the wrist, where it forms the wrist joint.

This phalanx (toe bone) is one of 14, with three phalanges in each toe except the big toe, which has two.

The femur (thighbone) forms the knee joint with the tibia and, at its upper end, has a rounded head that fits into a socket in the pelvic girdle.

The tibia (shinbone), the larger of the two bones in the lower leg, extends from the knee to the ankle and carries the weight of the body.

The calcaneus is the largest of the seven tarsal (ankle) bones in the foot and forms the heel.

All about bones

The bones that form the skeleton are living organs. Bones are constructed from bone tissue containing bone cells and matrix, a combination of flexible collagen fibers and hard calcium salts that makes bones springy yet tough. Bone tissue is denser on the outside of bones than on the inside, an arrangement that makes bones both strong and light.

Yellow bone marrow is a storehouse of fat that fills the central cavity of adult long bones. This space is occupied by red bone marrow in infants.

Blood vessels supply nutrients and oxygen to, and remove wastes from, the bone cells that shape and maintain bones.

Red bone marrow fills the spaces within spongy bone. It contains unspecialized stem cells that divide continuously to produce blood cells—red blood cells, white blood cells, and platelets.

The diaphysis, or shaft, of a long bone links its two epiphyses and consists mainly of compact bone and bone marrow.

RESHAPING BONES

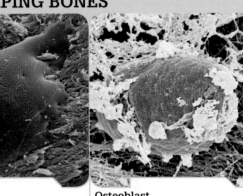

Osteoclast
Bones are constantly being reshaped by two types of cells, called osteoclasts and osteoblasts. Osteoclasts, such as this one, eat away at bone matrix.

Osteoblast
These cells build up bones by laying down bone matrix. Together, osteoclasts and osteoblasts ensure that bones are shaped to give them maximum strength.

The epiphysis is the expanded end or head of a long bone, such as the femur. It contains mainly spongy bone.

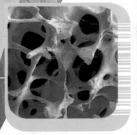

Spongy, or cancellous, bone consists of a honeycomb network of bony struts arranged along lines of greatest stress and separated by a maze of tiny spaces.

Bones in old skeletons appear dry and dusty, but living bones are 22 percent water.

An osteon is one of the cylindrical units, each consisting of concentric tubes of bone matrix, that make up compact bone. Its central canal carries blood vessels.

INSIDE BONES

This view inside a long bone, such as the femur, reveals its structure. Its outer layer consists of hard compact bone made of weight-bearing pillars called osteons that run in parallel along the bone's shaft. Beneath the compact bone layer, the network of open struts that makes up spongy bone is both light and strong. The cavity in the center of the shaft contains soft marrow tissue.

Compact bone, made up of parallel osteons, forms the hard, dense outer layer of the bone, which bears the most stress.

LOW GRAVITY

This astronaut is moving with ease because the Moon's gravity is just one-sixth that of the Earth. Gravity is the force that pulls us downward and gives our body weight. When we walk or run, our bones resist this downward pull, constantly reshaping themselves so they are strong enough to support the body's weight. On the Moon, low gravity makes the body almost weightless and an astronaut's bones become weaker and less dense.

The periosteum is a thin, tough membrane that covers the bone's surface (except at joints). It provides an attachment point for tendons and is essential for bone growth and repair.

Osteocytes, such as this one (purple), are widely spaced bone cells that live in isolation and are responsible for maintaining bone matrix.

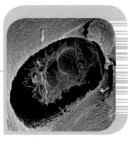

REPAIRING FRACTURES

Although bones are very strong, they sometimes fracture or break. A fractured bone repairs itself by producing new tissue to connect the broken ends. Doctors usually immobilize a fracture using a cast to aid healing. In severe cases, such as this broken thighbone, pins are inserted to line up the bone ends.

Pound for pound, bone is six times stronger than steel.

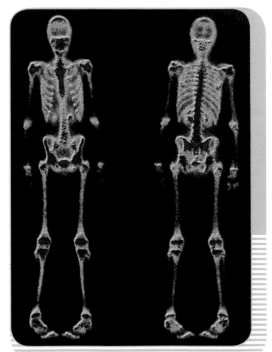

BONE SCAN

These radionuclide scans show front (left) and back views of a healthy skeleton. These scans pinpoint areas of bone tissue that are most active (red) and least active (blue). They can also detect activity that may indicate disease.

Flexible joints

Without joints, the skeleton would be rigid and movement would be impossible. Joints are located where two or more bones meet. Most, such as the knee, are free-moving synovial joints. Other types of joints, such as those between the vertebrae, are less versatile. Joints also help hold bones together.

In a ball-and-socket joint (light green), the ball-like end of one bone fits into the cup-shaped cavity of another bone, allowing a wide range of movements.

One of two bones that fit together in this synovial joint

Tough, fibrous capsule, aided by ligaments, holds joint together

Synovial membrane lining the joint capsule produces synovial fluid

Synovial fluid fills the small space between bones and aids lubrication

Glassy hyaline cartilage covers end of the bone

SMOOTH MOVER

In a synovial joint (above), bone ends are capped with slippery cartilage and separated by a narrow cavity filled with oily synovial fluid. Together, cartilage and fluid lubricate the joint and make it move smoothly.

With bone ends that fit together like paired saddles, the saddle joint (orange) at the base of the thumb allows movement back and forth and side to side.

In the ellipsoidal joints (blue) of the knuckles and wrists, the egg-shaped dome of one bone fits into a recess in another, allowing circular, up-and-down, and side-to-side movements.

DOUBLE-JOINTED

People described as being "double-jointed" can bend their bodies in ways that others would find impossible. This doesn't mean that they have twice the normal number of joints. Instead, their ligaments are unusually stretchy, making their joints much more flexible.

There are around 400 joints in the body. More than 250 are free-moving synovial joints.

SIX TYPES

Although all synovial joints share the same basic structure, they are divided into six types (ball-and-socket, saddle, ellipsoidal, plane, hinge, and pivot) according to how their bones fit together. This, in turn, determines the kinds of movements each allows. Here you can see how the shapes of bone ends allow different movements in each type of joint. The color-coded map shows where each type of joint is located in the body.

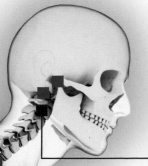

In a pivot joint (pink), a projection from one bone rotates within another bone. A pivot joint between the top two vertebrae allows the head to shake to indicate "No."

Around one-third of the body's joints are not free-moving synovial joints. These include the semi-movable joints between vertebrae, the bones that make up the backbone (right). Vertebrae are separated by intervertebral disks (blue) made of cartilage. Disks allow limited movement between pairs of vertebrae, and moving together they give the backbone flexibility, allowing the body to bend and twist. Disks also act as shock absorbers when the body is running or jumping.

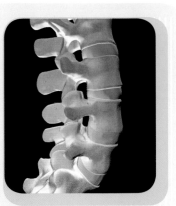

STRAPPED TOGETHER

Many joints are reinforced by ligaments (strong straps that hold bone ends together). Made from extra-tough collagen fibers, ligaments allow a joint to move but, not being stretchy, keep bones from being pulled apart. The hip joint (right) is big, freely movable, bears the body's weight, and is reinforced by several ligaments.

The femur (thighbone) forms a ball-and-socket joint with the hip bone that allows a wide range of movements.

Hinge joints (dark green) work like door hinges, allowing movement in just one direction. Found in the elbows, knees, fingers, and toes, they can only bend and straighten.

The hip bone forms one half of the pelvic girdle that connects the femur to the backbone.

Five ligaments hold together the ball-and-socket joint between the pelvic bone and femur, and prevent dislocation.

LOOKING INSIDE

These doctors are investigating a problem inside a knee joint using an arthroscope. This is a special type of endoscope (viewing tube) that is inserted through an incision into the patient's knee. The image on screen shows a view inside the joint, allowing the doctors to treat any problems.

OUT OF LINE

A sudden wrench or blow may force bones out of line so that the synovial joint between them becomes dislocated. Dislocations are often caused by falls or sports injuries. Doctors treat them by moving the bones back into their correct positions.

The flat bone surfaces in plane joints (purple) allow only limited gliding movements. They are found in the heels and palms, where stability is important.

This X-ray of a finger shows a dislocated knuckle joint where two bones have been wrenched apart.

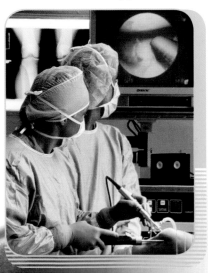

Muscle mass

The body's muscles possess a unique ability to contract and create a pulling force. Skeletal muscle, which makes up nearly 50 percent of our body weight, pulls the skeleton to make us move. Smooth muscle inside the body organs produces squeezing movements, while cardiac muscle in the heart pumps blood.

All skeletal muscle is made up of long, cylindrical cells called fibers (above) that run in parallel along the muscle. These fibers contract when instructed to by nerve signals received from the brain.

The splenius capitis muscles act together to pull the head backward or, acting singly, turn and bend the head to one side.

The deltoid raises the arm sideways away from the body and swings it backward and forward.

The erector spinae is a group of three muscles that straighten the back and help maintain upright posture.

The triceps brachii straightens the arm at the elbow and helps pull the arm toward the body.

The semimembranosus is one of the hamstrings—three muscles that straighten the thigh at the hip and bend the knee.

MAKING FACES

Frontalis raises the eyebrows

Orbicularis oris purses the lips

Relaxed expression
Facial expressions communicate our emotions to others. They are made by around 30 muscles, such as the frontalis and orbicularis oris, each of which pulls a small area of skin.

Levator labii superioris

Zygomaticus muscles

Risorius

Smiling
A smile involves the zygomaticus and risorius muscles pulling the corners of the mouth outward and upward, and the levator labii superioris lifting the upper lip.

Corrugator supercilii

Orbicularis oculi narrows the eye

Depressor muscles

Frowning
Frowns are produced when the corrugator supercilii muscles pull down and wrinkle the eyebrows. The depressor muscles pull the corners of the mouth downward.

TONE AND POSTURE
In addition to moving us, skeletal muscles—mainly those in the neck, back, and legs—maintain body posture, keeping us upright whether we are sitting, standing, or moving. When we sleep, those muscles relax. That's why, if someone falls asleep in a sitting position, their body lolls to one side.

The bulkiest muscle is the gluteus maximus in the buttocks. We use it to extend the thigh and push off when climbing or running.

BODY MOVERS
These front and back views of the male body show some of its 650 skeletal muscles. Muscles are arranged in layers that overlap each other, with superficial (surface) muscles overlying deep muscle. Superficial muscles are shown on the right side of each image, with deep muscles on the left. Muscles are given Latin names according to their location, size, shape, or action.

The abductor digiti minimi is a small muscle in the sole of the foot that pulls the little toe outward.

The masseter pulls the lower jaw upward during chewing, generating the pressure needed to crush food between the teeth.

The trapezius is a triangular muscle that moves the shoulder blade and helps pull the head backward.

The pectoralis major pulls the arm forward. It also draws it toward the body and rotates it inward.

BODYBUILDERS

Some men and women, known as bodybuilders, use special diets and intensive weight-training exercises to "pump up" their skeletal muscles so they are much bigger and better defined than normal. This bodybuilder's right arm shows his bulging biceps brachii muscle.

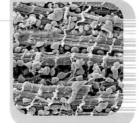

Cardiac muscle is found in the heart wall where its branching fibers (brown) form a network that contracts automatically around 100,000 times daily to pump blood.

Smooth muscle fibers (below) are found in the walls of hollow organs. They contract under unconscious control— for example, to push urine out of the bladder.

The biceps brachii bends the arm at the elbow and rotates the forearm to turn the palm upward.

The gluteus maximus is a powerful muscle that forcefully straightens the thigh at the hip in a thrusting movement during climbing or running.

The adductor longus rotates and pulls the thigh inward toward the body and helps bend the thigh at the hip.

The quadriceps femoris is a group of four powerful thigh muscles that straighten the leg at the knee.

HEAT GENERATORS

When muscles contract, they generate heat that keeps the body warm. Heat is lost through the skin as shown by this thermogram, or "heat picture," of a man exercising. Colors show which areas are radiating the most heat, ranging from the hottest (white), through red, yellow, and green, to the coolest (blue).

The gastrocnemius is the fleshy calf muscle that bends the foot downward— for example, when we walk or stand on tiptoe.

The tibialis anterior bends the foot upward and turns it inward. It also supports the foot's arch during running or walking.

The Achilles (calcaneal) tendon, the body's largest tendon, attaches the calf muscles, which bend the ankle, to the heel bone.

On the move

The muscles that move the body have a very precise structure that enables them to use energy in order to contract powerfully and efficiently when instructed to do so by the brain. Skeletal muscles exert their pulling power through the tough tendons that attach them to bones.

GETTING SHORTER

Inside a myofibril, thick and thin filaments are arranged in contraction units called sarcomeres. At rest, the actin filaments and the myosin filaments overlap slightly. When instructions arrive from the brain, the myosin heads attach to and pull the actin filaments. The sarcomeres shorten and the muscle fiber contracts.

Z band at end of each sarcomere

Thick myosin filament

M band

Myosin head

Thin actin filament

Relaxed   **Contracted**

Sarcomere gets shorter as filaments slide over each other

Blood capillaries supply oxygen and glucose that release energy for contraction.

A nerve-muscle junction is the interface between the end branches of a neuron (yellow) and muscle fibers (red). The neuron carries the signals that instruct the fibers to contract.

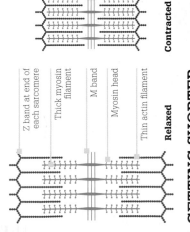

The perimysium is a tough sheath that surrounds each fascicle, holding muscle fibers together like a bundle of sticks.

WORKING IN PAIRS

Biceps relaxed

Triceps contracted

Forearm lowered

Straightening
To straighten the arm at the elbow, the biceps relaxes, while its partner, the triceps, gets shorter and fatter as it contracts to pull the forearm downward.

Biceps contracted

Triceps relaxed

Forearm raised

Bending
Muscles are arranged in pairs that have opposite actions. In the arm, for example, the biceps contracts to bend the elbow while the opposing triceps relaxes.

A fascicle is one of several bundles of long, parallel muscle fibers that together make up a skeletal muscle.

The epimysium is the protective "overcoat" that is wrapped around the outside of the whole muscle.

Skeletal muscle is an organ that is constructed from muscular, connective, and other tissues. It contracts to move the body.

INSIDE MUSCLES

This exploded view, which shows the highly ordered structure of a muscle, helps us understand how it contracts. Bundles of hundreds of muscle fibers (cells) run in parallel along the length of the muscle. Each fiber is packed with rodlike myofibrils, which, in turn, contain protein filaments that cause contraction. In addition, muscles contain blood vessels, nerves, and the connective tissue that holds them together.

MUSCLE ANCHORS

Tendons are strong cords that anchor muscles to bones. Tendons ensure that muscles can pull bones without tearing. As this cross section shows, tendons are packed with parallel bundles of tough collagen fibers (brown) that are secreted by cells called fibroblasts (purple). The fibers are embedded in the hard outer layer of the bone to form a very strong attachment.

A muscle fiber is one of the long, thin, cylindrical cells that has a striped appearance and makes up a muscle.

Myofibril is one of the parallel, rodlike strands that are packed inside each muscle fiber.

MOVEMENT AND EXERCISE

Regular exercise, such as running or swimming, improves the efficiency of skeletal muscles by increasing their blood supply and the size of muscle fibers. This, in turn, increases stamina and overall body fitness.

Sarcomere is one of the repeating patterns of filaments that give the myofibril and muscle fiber their striped appearance.

Filaments of actin and myosin (red and blue), shown in cross section, are highly organized inside the myofibril.

MOVING FINGERS

The slender forearm muscles that move the fingers taper into long tendons that cross the wrist. Muscles in the front of the forearm bend the fingers, while those in the back straighten the fingers.

The thin filaments inside each myofibril are made of twisted strands of the protein actin.

The thick filaments inside each myofibril are made from molecules of the protein myosin.

The head of a myosin molecule projects from the thick filament and interacts with the thin filament to cause contraction.

Tendon sheath is a long bag containing lubrication that wraps around the long tendon and keeps it from rubbing against bone

Tendons of the extensor digitorum muscle pass across the back of the hand and are attached to the end phalanges (finger bones) of each of the four fingers

Extensor retinaculum is a "wristband" that encloses the tendons running to the back of the hand and keeps them close to the wrist

Extensor digitorum muscle in the back of the forearm straightens the four fingers, which it is attached to by long tendons

Muscles can pull, but they cannot push.

Control

Nerve cells in the brain

The brain controls the body and makes it work. Day and night, the network of interlinked brain cells buzzes with continuous activity. Brain cells are constantly updated by the eyes, ears, and other sensors about what's happening inside and outside the body. They issue instructions—for example, to muscles to move the legs or to the heart to speed up—and, of course, these brainy cells give us our personality.

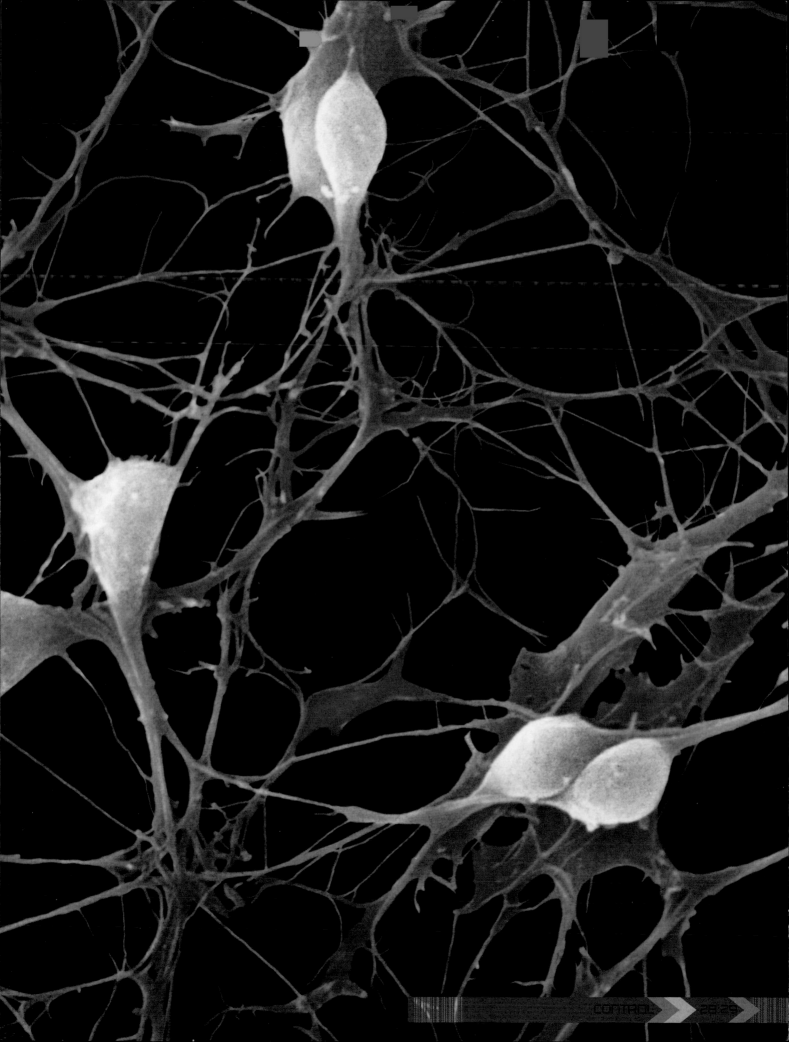

Brain power

The control center of the nervous system, the human brain possesses a processing power that is beyond compare. It makes us who we are, enabling us to think, be self-aware, imagine, remember, understand, see, feel, and move. It also controls essential functions such as heart rate and body temperature without us being aware of it.

The primary motor cortex sends signals to the body's skeletal muscles, instructing them to contract and move the body.

The premotor cortex, aided by the cerebellum, plans, guides, and coordinates complex movements such as playing a guitar or driving a car.

Planning

Thinking

Judging

The prefrontal cortex is involved in thinking, learning, understanding, problem solving, imagination, emotions, and personality.

Feeling

Speech

Taste

Smell

Mem

Broca's area, usually found on the left side of the cerebrum, controls the production of speech by the larynx, tongue, and lips; and the clear pronunciation of words.

The cerebral cortex (gray matter) is the thin, outer layer of the entire cerebrum—shown in brown on this brain section—where tasks such as feeling and thinking are performed.

The primary auditory cortex makes hearing possible by receiving and processing signals arriving from sound receptors in both ears.

The auditory association area analyzes sound input and compares it with memories to identify sounds and their sources.

BRAIN IN ACTION

See the brain light up

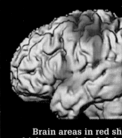

Brain areas in red show which parts of the left brain are active when a right finger moves

1 This special type of MRI scan shows the areas of the left cerebral cortex that are active (in red) when a specific movement is performed. Parts of the premotor cortex and the primary motor cortex have lit up as has the cerebellum, which is responsible for coordinating movements.

LEFT AND RIGHT

Get inside the cerebrum

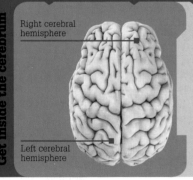

Right cerebral hemisphere

Left cerebral hemisphere

2 The brain's cerebrum is divided into two linked hemispheres. The left hemisphere controls the right half of the body and the right hemisphere controls the left half. The left side also handles language and math skills, while the right side deals with creativity and spatial awareness.

INSIDE THE BRAIN

This exploded view of the brain shows the two halves of the cerebrum surrounding the thalamus (which relays signals to the cerebrum), the hypothalamus (which regulates many internal activities), and the hippocampus (which helps create memories). The brain stem controls vital functions, such as breathing. The cerebellum coordinates body movements and balance.

Right cerebral hemisphere

Thalamus

Hypothalamus

Left cerebral hemisphere

Cerebellum

Hippocampus

Nerves

Brain stem

Spinal cord relays signals to and from brain

The human brain is the most complex organ in the world.

The primary sensory cortex makes detecting touch possible by receiving signals from the skin's sensory receptors.

The sensory association cortex processes, interprets, and compares skin sensations and stores them in memory.

Movement

Touch

Spatial awareness

Sound

Comprehension

Recognition

Visual processing

Vision

Cerebellum
(Coordination)

The primary visual cortex makes vision possible by receiving signals from the eyes that are generated when light strikes receptors in the retina.

Wernicke's area receives input from auditory and visual parts of the cortex. It enables the understanding of spoken and written language.

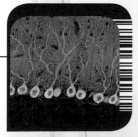

Pictured above are some of the 100 billion neurons (green) that are each linked to hundreds or thousands of other neurons to form a processing and communication network across the whole brain.

MAP OF THE CORTEX

The largest and most important part of the brain is the cerebrum. Its outer layer, the cerebral cortex, is packed with neurons that receive and process information and send out instructions. Distinct areas of the cortex carry out specific roles that are shown on this "brain map." Different areas also cooperate and interact with each other.

The visual association cortex analyzes incoming visual information and compares it with other senses and memories to create images.

BLOOD SUPPLY

This angiogram reveals the network of blood vessels that supply the brain with oxygen. Although it makes up just two percent of our body weight, the energy-hungry brain needs 20 percent of the body's oxygen intake at all times to release energy from glucose.

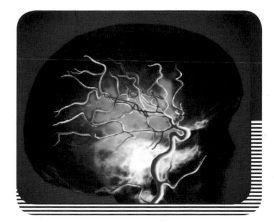

BRAIN WAVES

Every second, millions of nerve impulses speed through the brain's network of neurons. This creates patterns of electrical activity that can be detected by electrodes (left) and displayed as brain waves by a machine called an EEG. Brain waves vary according to whether we are awake or asleep.

REMEMBER THIS

Procedural memory
The brain's lifetime information storehouse, its long-term memory, has three basic types. Procedural memory involves skills learned by practice, such as playing tennis.

Semantic memory
Being able to store and retrieve information is essential for learning and creativity. Semantic memory deals with words, language, facts, rules, meanings, and knowledge.

Episodic memory
Only about one percent of our experiences make it into long-term memory. Episodic memory records specific events such as taking a trip or attending a wedding.

Nerve network

From running to thinking, seeing to breathing, body activities are controlled by the nervous system. It extends throughout the body, and is made up of billions of interconnected neurons that carry tiny electrical signals at high speed. Most neurons are packed into the brain and spinal cord. The remainder are bundled into nerves.

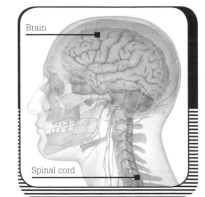

Brain

Spinal cord

CENTRAL NERVOUS SYSTEM (CNS)

Made up of the brain and spinal cord, the CNS controls and coordinates most body activities. It receives and processes information from sense organs and other receptors, and sends out instructions to muscles, glands, and other organs.

The radial nerve controls muscles in the back of the upper arm, forearm, and hand.

The ulnar nerve supplies some muscles that bend the wrist and fingers.

PERIPHERAL NERVOUS SYSTEM (PNS)

Sensory division
The PNS consists of neurons inside nerves that relay signals between the body and the CNS. It has three divisions. The sensory division carries information from sensors such as the eyes to the CNS.

Somatic division
Both somatic and autonomic divisions carry impulses from the CNS to the body. The somatic division instructs skeletal muscle to contract to move body parts, such as the fingers.

Autonomic division
Automatically and without us being aware of it, the autonomic division carries signals to internal organs to control their activities. One of its roles is to speed up or slow down heart rate.

Axon carries nerve impulses away from neuron's cell body and may be surrounded by insulating sheath cells that speed up transmission

Cell body of neuron contains nucleus, mitochondria, and other organelles

Synapse is the junction between the axon of one neuron and dendrite of a second

Dendrite receives signals from other neurons and carries nerve impulses toward cell body

IMPULSE CARRIERS
Neurons are adapted to generate and transmit electrical signals called nerve impulses at high speed. Short filaments called dendrites receive impulses from other neurons, while a long, thin filament called the axon transmits those signals to other neurons or to muscles.

The fastest neurons can transmit impulses at up to 217 mph (350 kph).

WIRED UP
You can see here how the nervous system (yellow) extends to all parts of the body from the scalp to the toes. At its core are the brain and spinal cord, which receive information about what is happening inside and outside the body, then process and respond to it. The network of cablelike nerves that arise from the brain and spinal cord send out branches that, for example, relay signals from sensory receptors or instruct muscles to contract.

Two of our billions of neurons, each linked to thousands of other neurons by fine connections that form the brain's control and communication network.

MAKING CONTACT

Where two neurons meet at a synapse (right), they are separated by a tiny gap. A nerve impulse reaching the end of the first neuron triggers the release of transmitter chemicals that pass across the gap and make the second neuron "fire."

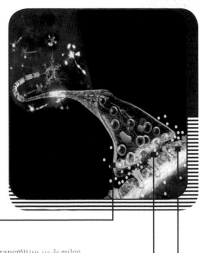

Axon of first neuron

Transmitter molecules pass across gap

Cell membrane of second neuron

This neuron is in a dorsal root ganglion, a swelling of nerve cells just outside the spinal cord that processes signals arriving from sensory receptors.

SUPPORT CELLS

The majority of cells that make up the nervous system are not neurons but glial cells, such as these astrocytes (green), that support and protect neurons. Astrocytes are star-shaped cells found in the brain and spinal cord that supply neurons with nutrients. Other types of glial cells include those that wrap themselves around the axons of neurons to provide insulation and those that trap invading bacteria.

A nerve-muscle junction between the ends of an axon (yellow) and skeletal muscle fibers (red). Impulses received through the junction make muscle fibers contract.

The sciatic nerve, the body's thickest and longest nerve, supplies the hamstring muscles at the back of the thigh. Its branches control muscles in the lower leg and foot.

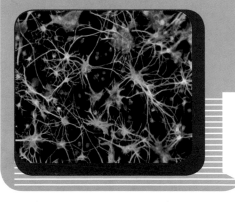

Nerves are made of bundles of axons, the long extensions of neurons. Seen in cross section, each axon (purple) is wrapped in a fatty sheath (red) that insulates and protects it.

This cross section of a nerve shows a tough, flexible sheath (purple) that surrounds a group of axons (red) to form a fascicle.

INSIDE A NERVE

Nerves are packed with millions of axons or nerve fibers that are bundled into fascicles. These fascicles, in turn, are enclosed by the nerve's outer sheath, which is protective, but also allows the nerve to bend when the body moves.

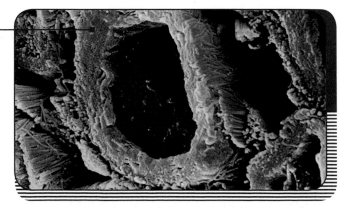

Touch and pain

We can experience the softness of velvet, the warmth of a hot shower, or the pain of a paper cut because of our largest sense organ, the skin. Within the skin, an array of touch receptors send signals to the sensory area of the brain to give us a "touch picture" of our surroundings.

The epidermis is the upper, thinner layer of the skin. Its surface is constantly lost as skin flakes and is replaced by cells migrating from below.

The hand of the homunculus is completely out of proportion because it has many touch receptors and a much larger brain area to process their signals.

A Meissner's corpuscle consists of a mass of nerve endings. It is common in sensitive, hairless skin, such as the fingertips, and detects light touch and pressure.

HOW SENSITIVE?

Some parts of the body, such as the lips, are more sensitive than others because they have far more touch receptors. In addition, bigger areas of the brain's sensory cortex are needed to process signals from more sensitive areas. This weird-looking "homunculus" shows body parts sized according to their sensitivity.

The dermis is the lower, thicker layer of the skin. It is made of connective tissue and contains most touch receptors, along with blood vessels and nerves.

Blood vessels supply oxygen and nutrients to all parts of the dermis, including the touch receptors, and also indirectly to living cells in the epidermis.

TOUCH READING

The skin of the fingertips has a greater concentration of the receptors that detect light touch than other body regions. The Braille reading system used by people who are blind exploits this sensitivity. Groups of raised dots (right) that represent letters and other symbols are "read" as the fingertips move over and touch them.

A Pacinian corpuscle is big, with a nerve ending surrounded by an "onion skin" of flattened cells. When squashed, it detects firm pressure and vibrations.

A nerve fiber carries nerve impulses, generated by a receptor when stimulated, toward the brain where those signals are interpreted.

A Merkel's disk in the upper dermis or lower epidermis has branched nerve endings associated with special disklike cells, and detects light pressure and touch.

FEELING PAIN

It may not be pleasant, but pain provides a warning signal that the body has been, or is at risk of being, injured or harmed in some way. Pain is triggered by receptors called nociceptors that detect intense pressure, burning heat, extreme cold, or chemicals released by damaged cells. Nociceptors are found not only in the skin, but also in internal organs, muscles, and joints.

Free nerve endings can extend into the epidermis, and may be thermoreceptors that detect heat or cold, or nociceptors that detect pain.

A Ruffini's corpuscle in the middle of the dermis responds to deep, continuous pressure, and to the stretching of the skin when objects slide across its surface.

PHANTOM FEELING

People who have had an arm or leg amputated sometimes feel that the limb is still there. They experience pain, tingling, and other sensations in the "phantom" limb. This happens because some of the limb's nerves remain, and send signals to the brain that are interpreted as phantom feelings.

SKIN RECEPTORS

As this cross section shows, the skin contains several types of sensory receptors. Each is located at a certain depth, usually in the dermis, that suits its role, whether it detects light touch, like a Merkel's disk, or deep pressure, like a Pacinian corpuscle. Most receptors are mechanoreceptors that respond when pulled or squashed and send signals to the brain. Others detect changes in temperature or allow us to feel pain.

TEMPERATURE CHANGE

Plunge into icy water, like this brave swimmer, and you'll soon become aware of just how cold it is. Free nerve endings near the skin's surface detect sudden temperature changes. They also send signals to the brain's hypothalamus that cause it to reduce heat loss through the skin to keep body temperature from falling. Temperature receptors soon adapt so that the water no longer feels as freezing as it did originally.

Reflex actions

Although we are individuals, we also show a range of inborn, split-second responses, often protective, that are the same in all of us. These are reflex actions, such as blinking or pulling the hand away from a hot object, that happen without our being aware of them. Many reflexes involve simple, high-speed nerve pathways that pass through the spinal cord.

As part of the swimming reflex, the baby's epiglottis automatically blocks the entrance to the trachea so that no water can get down to her lungs.

PULLING AWAY

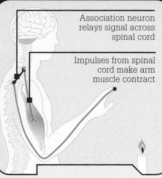

Nerve impulses from pain receptor travel to spinal cord

Association neuron relays signal across spinal cord

Impulses from spinal cord make arm muscle contract

Signal reaches brain and person feels pain

Harmful stimulus
A withdrawal reflex follows a simple path. The candle flame's heat stimulates pain receptors that send signals along sensory neurons (green) to the spinal cord.

Automatic withdrawal
An association neuron (red) in the spinal cord relays nerve signals to a motor neuron (blue). This carries the message instructing an upper arm muscle to pull the hand away.

Feeling pain
Once the hand is pulled away from harm, signals are relayed up the spinal cord to the brain. Only now does a person feel pain and become aware of what has happened.

Reflexes are automatic, unchanging, unconscious responses.

Gray matter processes incoming messages from receptors carried by sensory neurons and sends out instructions to muscles along motor neurons.

Spinal cord consists of gray matter surrounded by white matter, which contains axons that relay signals to and from the brain.

The column of vertebrae that make up the backbone forms a "tunnel" that surrounds and protects the pencil-thick spinal cord.

Spinal nerves, which emerge from the spinal cord through spaces between adjacent vertebrae, contain both sensory and motor neurons.

PRESENT AT BIRTH
Babies are born with several reflexes that help them survive, but which fade within two years. The rooting instinct causes a baby to turn its head toward its mother's breast automatically when the side of its face is touched, while the sucking reflex makes the baby suck the nipple to get milk. Other reflexes include the swimming reflex, shown here, and the grasping reflex.

SPINAL CORD
Part of the central nervous system, the spinal cord is a column of nervous tissue that extends down the back from the base of the brain. The spinal cord relays signals between the brain and the body by way of the spinal nerves, and also controls many of the body's reflex actions.

KNEE TAP

Stretch reflexes help maintain body posture, automatically adjusting muscle tension to keep us upright. Doctors use a stretch reflex to make sure the spinal cord is not damaged. A knee tap stretches a receptor inside the thigh muscle. In response, the spinal cord makes the thigh muscle contract, so the lower leg automatically kicks forward.

Placed in water, the baby begins to kick with her feet and paddle with her hands—a swimming reflex also triggered if she accidentally falls into water.

Water supports the weight of the baby's body so that, although she cannot crawl unaided at this age, she can move her arms and legs freely to propel herself.

Another newborn reflex is the grasping reflex, which lasts for just three months and causes the baby's fingers to automatically wrap around any object placed in the palm.

EYE PROTECTION

Three reflex actions protect the eyes from injury. Flying insects and bright light, for example, trigger reflex blinking that closes the eyelids. Fast-moving, larger objects approaching the head set off a withdrawal reflex that pulls the head backward. In real emergencies, the hands lift to shield the face.

GAG REFLEX

If an object other than food touches the back of the mouth, it triggers an automatic contraction of the throat called the gag reflex. This keeps unwanted objects from going down the throat and possibly causing choking. Sword swallowers learn to suppress the gag reflex to get the sword down their throat and into the esophagus.

NOSE CLEARING

Sneezing is a reflex action that clears irritants, including dust and cold viruses, out of the nasal passageways. Receptors in the lining of the nasal cavity detect irritation and send signals to the sneezing center in the brain stem. This triggers an explosive sneeze that forces air and mucus out through the nostrils at high speed.

Tastes and smells

These closely linked senses detect chemicals: either food molecules dissolved in saliva (taste) or odor molecules in the air (smell). Smell is far more sensitive than taste. The nose detects thousands of odors, while the tongue picks out just five tastes. Together, these senses let us enjoy flavorful food, but also warn us of possible dangers.

The end of a smell receptor cell (blue) projects from the olfactory epithelium. It has a cluster of hairlike cilia that detect odor molecules in incoming air.

The olfactory bulb carries signals from the olfactory nerves to the front of the brain, where smells are interpreted.

Circumvallate papillae

Fungiform papillae

Spiky filiform papillae lack taste buds, but grip food during chewing and contain touch and temperature receptors. Here, they surround a fungiform papilla, which has taste buds.

Opening to a taste bud

TONGUE AND TASTE

Your tongue's upper surface is covered with tiny bumps called papillae. Two types of papillae, fungiform (mushroom-shaped) and circumvallate (at the back of the tongue), house the taste buds, which detect sweet, salty, sour, bitter, and umami (savory) tastes.

▶▶ SUPERTASTERS

Some people are born with heightened senses of taste and smell. These "supertasters" are far more sensitive to tastes and odors, an ability that can be refined through training so that they can detect subtle differences in scents and flavors. They may exploit their inherited skills professionally. Food tasters, for example, assess foodstuffs in terms of odors, tastes, and overall flavors, as well as their textures and appearances.

The nasal cavity connects the nostrils to the throat and contains "shelves" that make air carrying odor molecules swirl upward and past the smell receptors.

The tongue is a muscular organ that moves and mixes food during chewing, and also houses the receptors that detect the tastes of chewed food.

A branch of the facial nerve carries nerve impulses from taste receptors in the front two-thirds of the tongue toward the brain.

There are around 1,000 different types of receptor cells in the nasal cavity. Between them, they can distinguish about 20,000 different odors.

Olfactory bulb relays signals from smell receptors to brain

Nerve fiber of olfactory nerve passes through channel in skull bone

Skull bone

Mucus-secreting gland

Olfactory (smell) receptor cell

Cilia projecting from tip of receptor cell

Air flow

Odor molecules (blue) dissolve in watery mucus (brown)

PATHWAYS TO THE BRAIN

The nasal cavity houses olfactory (smell) receptors and the mouth contains the tongue and taste buds. Signals from both are carried along nerves (green) to the brain. Smell signals travel to the olfactory cortex and to the brain's limbic system (important in memory and emotions), which explains why some smells create strong feelings. Taste signals pass along two nerves toward the gustatory (taste) areas of the cortex.

ODOR DETECTORS

The olfactory epithelium (blue) at the top of the nasal cavity contains odor detectors. Odor molecules dissolve in watery mucus covering the epithelium's surface. Here, they are detected by cilia projecting from the ends of smell receptor cells. These fire off signals to the brain, which identifies the specific odor.

The brain stem receives nerve signals from the tongue through the facial and glossopharyngeal nerves and sends them to the areas of the brain where tastes are identified.

The glossopharyngeal nerve carries signals from the rear one-third of the tongue.

WORKING TOGETHER

Warning signs
Our senses of smell and taste also warn us about dangers. Foods that taste sour or bitter may be rotten or poisonous. Detecting smells such as smoke may protect us from harm.

Great flavors
When we eat, the brain combines smell and taste signals to give us an appreciation of flavors. When we're hungry, great flavors increase our enjoyment of food.

Communication
Smell is a vital communication tool for other mammals. In humans, it is more subtle, but we are attracted to partners who smell different from us because of genetic differences.

Sounds and balance

Our sense of hearing detects sound waves that pass through the air from a vibrating source, such as a plucked guitar string, to our ears. In addition to making us alert to different sounds, hearing allows us to communicate using speech. The ears also supply information to the brain that helps us maintain balance.

EARDRUM

The eardrum, or tympanum, is a thin membrane, as taut as a drum skin, that separates the outer and middle parts of the ear. Its inner surface (shown here) is joined to the hammer (malleus), one of the ossicles. Sounds from outside the body make the eardrum vibrate.

Anvil (incus)

Stirrup (stapes)

Hammer (malleus)

Semicircular canals inside the inner ear detect rotational movements of the head in every direction.

The ossicles are a chain of three bones that transmit sound vibrations.

The cochlear nerve carries nerve impulses from hair cells (sound detectors) in the cochlea to the auditory areas of the brain that identify sounds.

CHAIN OF BONES

The ossicles are three tiny bones that form a chain stretching from the eardrum to the oval window. Their individual names (Latin in parentheses) reflect their shapes. When sound waves make the eardrum vibrate, the ossicles transmit those movements to the oval window and into the inner ear.

The cochlea is a fluid-filled spiral chamber, coiled like a snail shell. It contains receptors that detect sound vibrations arriving from the oval window.

SOUND DETECTORS

Around 15,000 hair cells inside the cochlea detect sounds and send signals to the hearing area of the brain. Each cell is topped with a V-shaped tuft of "hairs" (yellow). Sound vibrations rippling through the fluid filling the cochlea bend these hairs and trigger the generation of nerve impulses.

INSIDE THE EAR

Except for the outer ear flaps, most of the ear is concealed and protected inside bones. The ear is divided into three sections—outer, middle, and inner. The outer ear collects sound waves and channels them toward the eardrum, making it vibrate. In the air-filled middle ear, three tiny linked bones transmit those vibrations to receptors inside the fluid-filled inner ear that send nerve impulses to the brain.

The eustachian tube links the ear to the throat, keeping air pressure the same inside the ear as outside the body.

The oval window is a membrane that forms the entrance to the fluid-filled inner ear.

These tiny calcium carbonate crystals cover, and add weight to, balance receptors in the utricle and saccule (see page 41, top right).

The stirrup, the body's smallest bone, is no bigger than a grain of rice.

STAYING BALANCED

Fluid-filled organs in the inner ear send signals to the brain to help us maintain balance. Semicircular canals detect the rotation of the head. The utricle and saccule detect the position of the head when stationary, and its acceleration in a straight line.

Three semicircular canals arranged at right angles to each other

Ampulla (bulge) contains receptors that detect movement of fluid when head moves

Utricle (left) and saccule contain receptors that detect head's position and movement

Vestibular nerve carries signals from balance receptors to brain

Scalp muscles (red) and fat tissue (yellow) around the outer part of the ear provide additional support.

Cartilage is the tough, bendy connective tissue that gives the ear's pinna a springy framework, supporting it and making it flexible.

The temporal bone is one of the skull bones that surrounds and protects the inner parts of the ear.

The outer ear canal carries sound waves toward the eardrum, and secretes earwax that cleans the canal and, with the help of short hairs, deters insects.

FEELING DIZZY

Spinning around and around makes us feel dizzy and sometimes sick. The act of spinning causes receptors in the ears and eyes to send conflicting messages to the brain that briefly upset the body's normal balance mechanism and make us feel unsteady. A similar but longer-lasting confusion of messages results in seasickness.

On a noisy street we are bombarded with sounds, but having two ears enables us to determine which direction those sounds are coming from. Usually, sounds reach one ear a split second before the other. This slight difference is used by the brain to figure out the source of the sound. Animals such as wolves and deer do this even more efficiently than we do, thanks to their long, movable ears.

Scalp muscle

The pinna, or ear flap, helps pick up sound waves from outside and direct them into the outer ear canal so they travel toward the eardrum.

In vision

The most important sense, vision gives us a clear impression of our surroundings. Light is detected by the eyes, complex organs that contain 70 percent of the body's sensory receptors. Signals from the eyes are interpreted by the brain to create moving, 3-D images.

INSIDE THE EYE

This cross section of the eye shows its key components. Light enters through the cornea at the front of the eye, passes through the pupil, and is focused onto the retina. Like a digital camera, the eye automatically adjusts its focusing mechanism to produce clear images of objects, regardless of their distance, and controls the amount of light entering the eye in response to changing light levels.

LIGHT RECEPTORS

This microscopic view of the retina shows its light receptors, called rods (blue) and cones (blue-green). The 130 million rods work best in dim light. The 6.5 million cones work best in bright light and detect color. When light hits the receptors, they generate signals that travel to the brain.

The pupil is a hole at the center of the iris that allows light to pass into the back part of the eye.

The cornea is a clear layer at the front of the eye that partially focuses light passing through it.

The iris is the colored part that controls the amount of light entering the eye by changing the pupil's size.

The lens is a transparent disk with curved surfaces that changes shape to focus light on the retina.

The ciliary body is a ring of muscle that surrounds the lens and contracts or relaxes to change its shape.

BRIGHT LIGHT

Decrease pupil

1 The pupil allows light to enter the eye. Its size is constantly adjusted by the iris as light levels change. In bright light, circular muscle fibers in the iris contract to make the pupil small, allowing less light into the eye so a person is not dazzled.

Circular muscle fibers contract to narrow pupil

DIM LIGHT

Increase pupil

2 The spokelike radial muscle fibers of the iris contract in dim light. This makes the pupil much wider, admitting the extra light that makes vision possible in dim conditions. Like the narrowing of the pupil in bright light, this is an automatic reflex action.

Radial muscle fibers contract to widen pupil

MOVE AND SCAN

The eyes are moved by six small muscles. Their contractions are coordinated to ensure that both eyeballs move together in the same direction. Eye muscles produce precise movements that allow the eyes to track objects on the move or to scan something, such as a face, that is stationary.

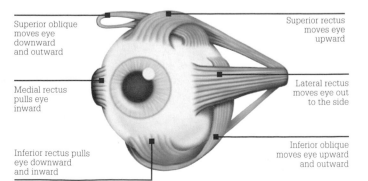

Superior oblique moves eye downward and outward

Superior rectus moves eye upward

Medial rectus pulls eye inward

Lateral rectus moves eye out to the side

Inferior rectus pulls eye downward and inward

Inferior oblique moves eye upward and outward

The fovea is a tiny part of the light-detecting retina (yellow layer) directly behind the lens that is packed with cones, enabling it to detect detailed images in color.

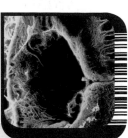

Visual cortex at the back of the brain processes signals from eyes

Thalamus relays signals from eyes to visual cortex

Right visual field is view of object seen by right eye

Optic nerve carries signals generated when light from object (butterfly) hits retina

Left visual field is view of object seen by left eye

BRAIN PATHWAYS

Although the eyes detect light, it is in the back of the brain that signals carried along pathways from the eyes are turned into images that we can "see." Each eye has a slightly different view of an object. By comparing these differences, the brain can judge distances and see objects in 3-D.

The eye can distinguish between up to 10 million different colors.

The sclera is the tough, protective outer layer of the eyeball.

The optic nerve carries nerve signals from the retina to the brain.

The vitreous humor is a jellylike liquid that shapes the eyeball.

IN FOCUS

3 Light rays are focused by the cornea and lens to produce a sharp image on the retina. The cornea does most of the focusing work but cannot change shape. The lens changes shape to focus light rays based on whether they are from near or distant objects.

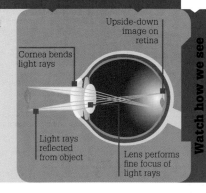

Upside-down image on retina

Cornea bends light rays

Light rays reflected from object

Lens performs fine focus of light rays

Watch how we see

TRICKS AND ILLUSIONS

Does this square have curved sides? Are the circles rotating? It might appear so, but in reality both are visual tricks. The brain uses clues to make sense of what it is seeing, but if they are confusing, the brain is tricked into drawing the wrong conclusions.

Tear gland produces tears to clean and moisten eye

Eyelids blink to sweep tears over eye's surface

Tear ducts empty tears onto surface of eyeball

Eyelashes help protect eye from foreign particles such as dust

Nasolacrimal duct drains tears from the eye into nasal cavity

EYE PROTECTION

Most of the eye is protected inside the bony eye socket. Its exposed part is protected by eyebrows, eyelids, and eyelashes that keep out sweat, dust, and excessive light. Blinking spreads tears across the eye's surface, washes away dust, and helps prevent infection.

Chemical messengers

The body's second control system, the endocrine system, works alongside the nervous system, but in a different way . Its endocrine glands release hormones—chemical messengers that travel in the blood to regulate specific target tissues. Hormones usually have long-lasting effects, controlling processes such as growth, metabolism, and reproduction.

The hypothalamus releases hormones that travel to the pituitary gland. It also links the endocrine and nervous systems.

The pineal gland releases melatonin that helps control the body's daily rhythms, such as sleeping and waking.

The pituitary gland releases a number of hormones, some of which control other endocrine glands.

The four small parathyroid glands are surrounded by the thyroid gland. Together, these five glands release hormones that control levels of calcium in the blood.

The thyroid gland also produces thyroxine, a hormone that regulates metabolic rate—the speed at which things work inside the body.

The thymus gland is most active in childhood. It produces hormones needed for the immune system to develop normally.

Hormones are broken down by the liver so that they have a limited lifespan.

Hypothalamus is a part of the brain that also controls many other things, including hunger and thirst

Neurosecretory cells release two hormones that travel to, and are stored by, the posterior pituitary

Anterior (front) lobe of pituitary gland makes eight hormones that affect reproduction, metabolism, and growth

Blood vessels carry releasing factors from hypothalamus that trigger release of anterior-lobe hormones

Posterior (back) lobe of pituitary stores and releases two hormones, one of which, ADH, controls urine production

HORMONE PRODUCERS

This map of the body shows many of the scattered organs that make up the endocrine system. Some, such as the pituitary, thyroid, and adrenal glands, are purely endocrine organs, the sole function of which is to release hormones. Others, such as the hypothalamus, pancreas, and ovaries, release hormones in addition to their other roles. Supervised by the hypothalamus, the pituitary gland is in overall control of many other endocrine glands.

HYPOTHALAMUS AND PITUITARY

Being closely connected, the hypothalamus and pituitary gland provide a key link between the nervous and hormonal systems. Although the pituitary gland controls many other endocrine glands, it relies on the neighboring hypothalamus to provide some of its hormones and to trigger the release of others.

The stomach releases hormones that stimulate the production and release of enzymes that aid digestion.

The pancreas releases two hormones, insulin and glucagon, that control glucose levels in the blood.

The adrenal glands release adrenaline, which helps the body deal with emergencies, and other hormones that regulate metabolism.

The kidneys release a hormone that stimulates red blood cell production, and another that helps regulate blood pressure.

The ovaries release the female sex hormones estrogen and progesterone, which maintain female features and stimulate egg ripening.

TESTES

In addition to producing sperm, the two testes also contain endocrine tissue that, when stimulated by pituitary gland hormones, release the male sex hormone testosterone. This produces and maintains male features and also encourages sperm production.

In times of threat, the hypothalamus fires up the autonomic nervous system (ANS) to prepare the body to confront danger or, as here, run away from it. In addition to increasing heart and breathing rates, releasing more fuel into the blood, and increasing blood flow to muscles, the ANS makes the adrenal glands release adrenaline—a hormone that reinforces the fight-or-flight response.

Stimulating release

Feedback mechanisms maintain the right levels of hormones in the blood. In the case of the hormone thyroxine, feedback involves two hormones (above) that regulate it.

Hypothalamus produces thyrotropin-releasing hormone (TRH)

Pituitary gland releases thyroid-stimulating hormone (TSH)

Too low

If levels of thyroxine are low, TRH production increases. This causes the pituitary gland to release more TSH, which stimulates the thyroid to make more thyroxine.

Trachea is straddled by thyroid gland

TSH stimulates thyroid gland

Too high

If high levels of thyroxine are detected by the hypothalamus, it cuts the production of TRH. This reduces TSH from the pituitary, so the thyroid makes less thyroxine.

Thyroid gland cells release thyroxine

Blood vessel carries thyroxine away

SLEEPING AND WAKING

Released during the hours of darkness, melatonin makes us sleep. Daylight stops its release, so we wake up. Long winter nights increase melatonin levels, sometimes causing a type of depression called seasonal affective disorder (SAD). Light therapy (right) can treat SAD because it inhibits melatonin release.

Maintenance

Lung cross section showing bronchus and pulmonary artery

Body cells are universally demanding. For them to work properly, those demands must be met. Cells need a constant supply of oxygen, brought into the body by the lungs, as well as food, water, and other essentials—not now and then, but all the time. They must also have their waste removed, be kept in constant conditions, and be protected from germs. This is what maintenance is all about.

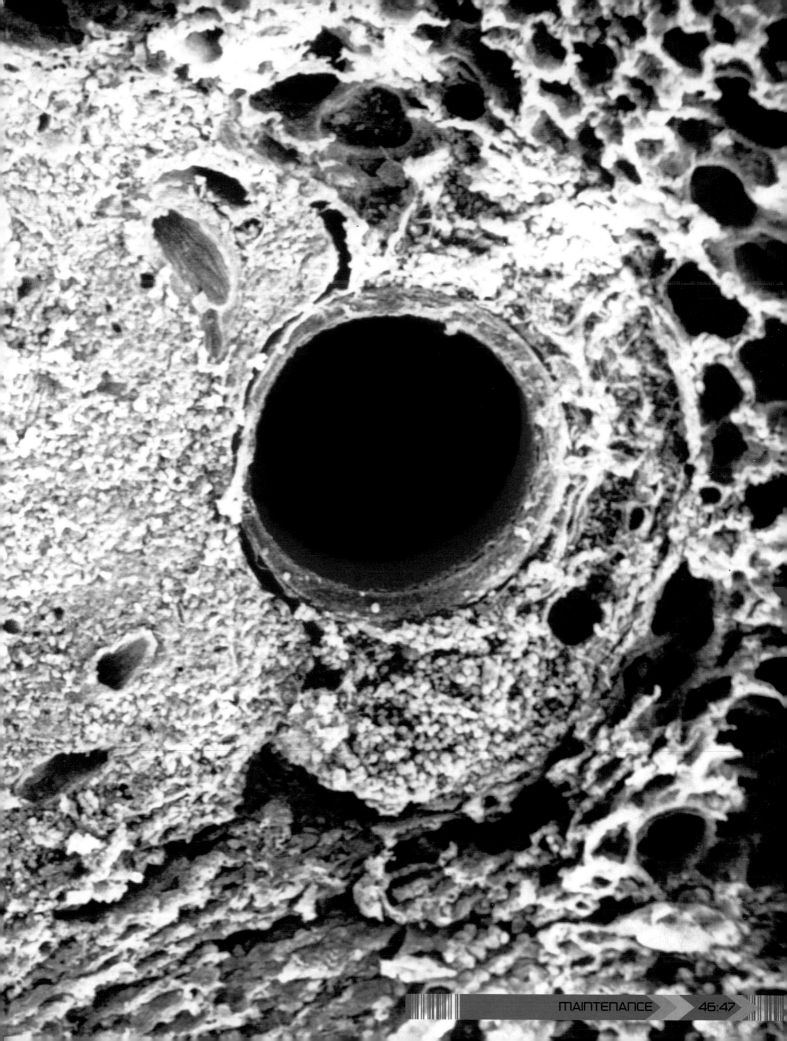

In the blood

Pumped along the network of blood vessels by the heart, this incredible red liquid supplies each one of the body's trillions of cells with oxygen, food, and other essentials, and removes their waste. Blood also helps defend the body against invasion by germs and keeps body temperature constant.

Red blood cells have a lifespan of 120 days, and a dimpled shape that makes taking up oxygen more efficient.

Also found in the lymphatic system, lymphocytes are white blood cells with large nucleii. They release chemicals called antibodies that disable pathogens, such as bacteria, and mark them for destruction.

BLOOD PARTS

Yellowish plasma, which makes up 55 percent of blood, is mainly water with many dissolved substances, including nutrients, wastes, and hormones. Floating in plasma are red blood cells (44 percent of blood) and white blood cells (one percent).

Plasma

Blood

Hemoglobin has four sites (yellow/green) for binding oxygen molecules

Oxygen molecules picked up by hemoglobin in lungs to make oxyhemoglobin

Hemoglobin

Interior of red blood cell packed with hemoglobin

Cross section of red blood cell shows its dimpled shape

Inside red blood cell

Oxyhemoglobin

Oxyhemoglobin contains four bound oxygen molecules

Oxygen molecules are released from oxyhemoglobin in tissues to make hemoglobin

OXYGEN CARRIERS

Unlike other body cells, red blood cells lack a nucleus and other organelles. Instead, each cell is packed with around 250,000 molecules of hemoglobin. This substance picks up oxygen where it is plentiful, in the lungs, and releases it where oxygen is scarce and in demand, in the tissues.

The lining of a blood vessel is smooth to allow blood to flow easily.

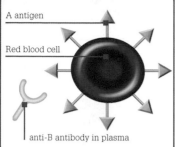

A antigen

Red blood cell

anti-B antibody in plasma

Blood type A
We each have one of four blood types—A, B, AB, or O—depending on which antigen (a marker that projects from red blood cells) is carried. Type A has A antigens.

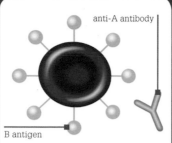

anti-A antibody

B antigen

Blood type B
Three of the blood types carry antibodies (proteins) in the plasma, which are usually the antibodies for the antigen they lack. Type B, for example, has anti-A antibodies.

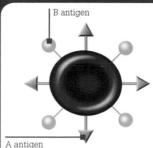

B antigen

A antigen

Blood type AB
Plasma may contain up to two antibodies that will bind to "foreign" antigens. However, type AB blood has no antibodies since it has both A and B antigens.

anti-A antibody

anti-B antibody

Blood type O
These blood cells carry neither A nor B antigens, but if blood cells carrying "foreign" antigens is transfused, antibodies cause them to clump together.

Neutrophils are white blood cells with a lobed nucleus that track down pathogens in the tissues, then engulf and destroy them.

CHANGING COLOR
As blood circulates around the body, its redness alters because the hemoglobin inside red blood cells changes color. After hemoglobin picks up oxygen in the lungs, blood passing through arteries is bright red. Once hemoglobin unloads oxygen in the tissues, blood traveling along veins is dark purple-red.

Oxygen-poor blood

Oxygen-rich blood

Blood makes up around eight percent of our body weight.

Platelets are cell fragments that play a key role in blood clotting. If a blood vessel is damaged, platelets stick together (blue) to plug the leak.

LIQUID TISSUE
This view of blood coursing along a blood vessel shows that it is a liquid tissue containing various cells. Red cells (which give blood its color) carry oxygen, white cells defend the body against pathogens, and platelets form clots. Around 10.5 pints (five liters) of blood circulate around the body of the average adult. A single drop of blood contains around 250 million red blood cells, 375,000 white blood cells, and 16 million platelets.

BLUE-BLOODED

In times past, having suntanned skin would mark you as being a poor peasant who labored all day unprotected from the sun. Spared from working outdoors, the rich and aristocratic were easily identified by their pale skin. Dark-red blood flowing through veins near the surface of pale skin gives them a dark blue appearance, hence the term "blue blooded" to describe the wealthy.

Beating heart

The power plant of the circulatory system, the heart is a muscular pump that pushes blood around the body to supply every cell with food and oxygen. Made of cardiac muscle, which contracts spontaneously and without tiring, the heart beats around 2.5 billion times in an average lifetime without taking a break.

The superior vena cava carries oxygen-poor blood from the head and upper body to the right atrium.

OUTSIDE VIEW

See inside the heart

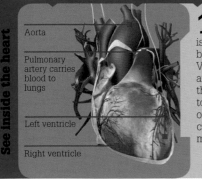

Aorta

Pulmonary artery carries blood to lungs

Left ventricle

Right ventricle

1 Around the size of its owner's fist, the heart is located in the chest between the two lungs. Visible from the outside are the muscular wall of the heart that contracts to pump blood, the outlines of the heart's chambers, and the heart's major blood vessels.

The heart pumps the body's blood volume, about 10.5 pints (5 liters), around the body once every minute.

HOW THE HEART BEATS

Make the heart beat

Blood flows in from lungs

Left atrium fills with blood

Right atrium fills with blood

Blood flows in from body

Right and left atria contract

Semilunar valves are closed

Valves open between atria and ventricles

Ventricles fill with blood

Blood pumped to body

Blood pumped to lungs

Semilunar valves open

Valves closed

Ventricles contract

2 Relaxed heart
Each heartbeat cycle has three stages controlled by the heart's own pacemaker. Initially, the atria and ventricles relax, and blood flows into both the right and left atria.

Atria contract
The right and left atria then contract, squeezing blood through open valves into the two ventricles. The semilunar valves remain closed, preventing backflow.

Ventricles contract
Finally, both ventricles contract, forcing blood out to the lungs and body. The blood pushes open the semilunar valves, but closes those between the atria and ventricles.

The right atrium receives oxygen-poor blood from the body.

The tricuspid valve prevents a backflow of blood from the right ventricle into the right atrium when the ventricle contracts.

The myocardium consists of cardiac muscle fibers (pink) supplied with energy by large mitochondria (blue/gold).

STOPPING BACKFLOW
During each heartbeat cycle, valves in the heart prevent blood from flowing in the wrong direction. These semilunar valves, which guard the exits from the right and left ventricles, open to let blood out of the heart when the ventricles contract, but close when the ventricles relax.

Valve flaps forced apart by pressure of blood

Higher blood pressure behind valve when heart pumps

Blood is trapped by closed valve and cannot flow backward

Valve flaps forced shut by pressure of blood in front of valve

Lower blood pressure behind valve when heart relaxes

The pericardium is a tough, two-layered bag that surrounds and protects the heart.

The inferior vena cava carries oxygen-poor blood from the lower body to the right atrium.

The aorta is the body's biggest artery. It carries oxygen-rich blood from the left ventricle to body tissues.

LISTENING TO THE HEART

A doctor uses a stethoscope to listen to a child's heart sounds, produced when heart valves close during each heartbeat. The valves between atria and ventricles make a long, loud "lub" sound, while semilunar valves make a short, sharp "dub" sound.

The pulmonary semilunar valve prevents a backflow of blood from the pulmonary artery into the right ventricle.

PARTS OF THE HEART

The heart is actually two pumps in one, with right and left sides. The right side receives oxygen-poor blood from the body and pumps it to the lungs to be enriched with oxygen. The left side receives oxygen-rich blood from the lungs and pumps it to the body. Each side has a smaller upper chamber, the atrium, linked to a larger lower chamber, the ventricle.

Right coronary artery branches from aorta to supply right side of heart

Aorta emerging from heart

Left coronary artery branches from aorta to supply left side of heart

FUEL SUPPLIES

Hardworking cardiac muscle needs a constant supply of glucose (fuel) and oxygen to release the energy needed to keep the heart beating. This is provided by blood flowing through a network of coronary blood vessels. The branches of coronary vessels (above) penetrate all parts of the heart's wall.

The left atrium receives oxygen-rich blood from the lungs.

The left ventricle pumps oxygen-rich blood to the body.

BLOOD PRESSURE

When the heart's ventricles contract and squeeze out blood, they generate the pressure that pushes blood around the body. Blood pressure can be measured using a sphygmomanometer (right). Higher-than-normal blood pressure can cause health problems.

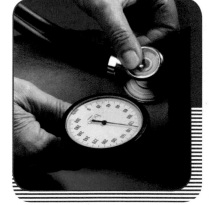

HEALTHY HEART

Regular exercise and a good diet help keep the heart healthy and working properly. Daily aerobic exercise such as walking, running, or swimming increases the strength of the heart, makes it pump more efficiently, and improves a person's stamina and fitness. A diet with plenty of fresh fruit and vegetables but low in junk food and animal fats will also benefit the heart.

Heartstrings are thin cords that anchor the valve between the atrium and the ventricle to the heart wall to keep it from turning inside out during contraction.

The right ventricle pumps oxygen-poor blood into the pulmonary artery for transport to the lungs.

Delivery system

To deliver supplies to cells, blood circulates in one direction through a massive network of living tubes called blood vessels. This delivery network, the circulatory system, contains three types of blood vessels. Arteries carry blood away from the heart, veins transport it toward the heart, and capillaries pass through tissues to link arteries to veins.

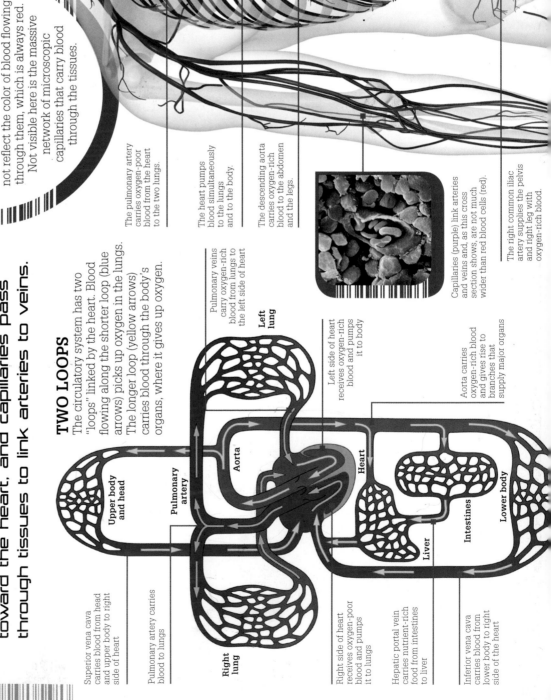

CIRCULATORY SYSTEM

This map of the human body shows its major blood vessels extending from the heart to all parts of the body, from the brain to the toes. Red is used to show arteries, and blue to show veins, although this does not reflect the color of blood flowing through them, which is always red. Not visible here is the massive network of microscopic capillaries that carry blood through the tissues.

The left common carotid artery branches from the aorta to carry oxygen and nutrients to the head and the brain.

The left subclavian vein drains oxygen-poor blood from the left arm and carries it toward the heart.

The pulmonary artery carries oxygen-poor blood from the heart to the two lungs.

The heart pumps blood simultaneously to the lungs and to the body.

The descending aorta carries oxygen-rich blood to the abdomen and the legs.

Capillaries (purple) link arteries and veins and, as this cross section shows, are not much wider than red blood cells (red).

The right common iliac artery supplies the pelvis and right leg with oxygen-rich blood.

TWO LOOPS

The circulatory system has two "loops" linked by the heart. Blood flowing along the shorter loop (blue arrows) picks up oxygen in the lungs. The longer loop (yellow arrows) carries blood through the body's organs, where it gives up oxygen.

Pulmonary veins carry oxygen-rich blood from lungs to the left side of heart

Left lung

Left side of heart receives oxygen-rich blood and pumps it to body

Aorta carries oxygen-rich blood and gives rise to branches that supply major organs

Upper body and head

Aorta

Pulmonary artery

Heart

Liver

Intestines

Lower body

Right lung

Superior vena cava carries blood from head and upper body to right side of heart

Pulmonary artery carries blood to lungs

Right side of heart receives oxygen-poor blood and pumps it to lungs

Hepatic portal vein carries nutrient-rich food from intestines to liver

Inferior vena cava carries blood from lower body to right side of the heart

TYPES OF BLOOD VESSELS

Thick muscle layer

Elastic layer

Inner lining

Artery
Carrying oxygen-rich blood from the heart, arteries have thick walls that are muscular and elastic to withstand the high blood pressure generated with every heartbeat.

Thin muscle layer

Valve prevents backflow

Vein
Carrying oxygen-poor blood under low pressure back to the heart, veins have thinner walls than arteries, and valves to keep blood from flowing in the wrong direction.

Very thin wall made of single cell layer

Capillary
Making up 98 percent of the total length of blood vessels, capillaries are microscopic with a thin, leaky wall through which oxygen and food pass to reach tissue cells.

Stretched out end to end, the body's blood vessels would extend for 62,000 miles (100,000 km).

The right femoral artery, the main artery of the upper leg, supplies the large muscles of the thigh as well as the knee.

The right femoral vein drains oxygen-poor blood from the thigh and carries it toward the heart.

SEEING BLOOD VESSELS

Doctors use several imaging techniques, including special types of X-rays, to look at blood vessels in a patient's body to make sure they are functioning normally and are not bulging, narrowed, or otherwise damaged. This MRA (magnetic resonance angiography) scan, for example, uses a form of MRI imaging to show healthy arteries (red) supplying the brain (blue).

CAPILLARY NETWORK

A vast network or bed of microscopic capillaries spreads through every tissue. This ensures that every cell is close to, and receives supplies from, a capillary. Capillaries arise from arterioles that branch from larger arteries. Having delivered oxygen and other essentials, capillaries merge into venules that drain into larger veins.

Artery carries oxygen-rich blood from heart into tissues, where it divides into arterioles

Arteriole is a very small artery, the diameter of which can be altered to control blood flow

Capillary bed is a network of microscopic blood vessels that passes close to every cell in tissues

Venule is a tiny vein that drains oxygen-poor blood from capillary network into vein

Vein carries blood away from tissues and connects with larger veins that eventually empty blood into heart

Vital defenses

The body is under constant threat from pathogens—microorganisms such as bacteria and viruses that cause disease if they get inside the body. The body has several lines of defense to protect itself from invasion, including physical barriers such as the skin, and the immune system, which consists of white blood cells, especially lymphocytes and macrophages.

DRAIN AND DEFEND

The lymphatic system is a one-way network of vessels (purple) that drains excess fluid—called lymph—from the tissues and returns it to the bloodstream. As lymph travels along lymph vessels, it passes through swellings called lymph nodes, where it is processed by immune system cells, lymphocytes and macrophages. Other linked lymphoid organs include the spleen and tonsils.

HIGH TEMPERATURE

This child is having his temperature checked using a thermometer. If infected by bacteria or viruses, the body often responds by increasing body temperature. This slows down pathogen multiplication, but increases the activity of white blood cells.

A ring of tonsils at the back of the mouth destroys bacteria carried in food or air.

The left subclavian vein is the blood vessel into which lymph empties from the thoracic duct.

The right lymphatic duct collects lymph from the upper right side of the body. It empties into the right subclavian vein (below).

The thymus gland "trains" T-lymphocytes (cells that play a key role in the immune system).

The spleen is the largest lymphoid organ. It contains pathogen-destroying lymphocytes and macrophages that engulf bacteria.

The thoracic duct collects lymph from the legs, abdomen, and left side of the body.

BARRIERS TO INFECTION

From the skin to tears, and stomach acid to mucus, the body's outer defenses are in place to keep pathogens from invading tissues or getting into the bloodstream. The main parts of those outer defenses are shown here.

Salivary glands release watery saliva that washes out the mouth to remove debris. Saliva also contains chemicals that destroy some types of bacteria.

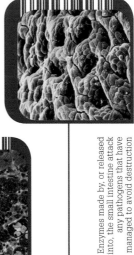

The lining of the stomach is pitted with glands that release gastric juice, a highly acidic liquid that kills almost all pathogens.

Enzymes made by, or released into, the small intestine attack any pathogens that have managed to avoid destruction in the acid-bath stomach.

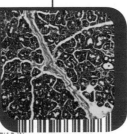

Tear glands release watery tears that wash away dust and pathogens with every blink. Tears also contain lysozyme, which destroys certain bacteria.

The trachea lining is covered with sticky mucus that traps pathogens that are moved by cilia (red) to the throat for swallowing.

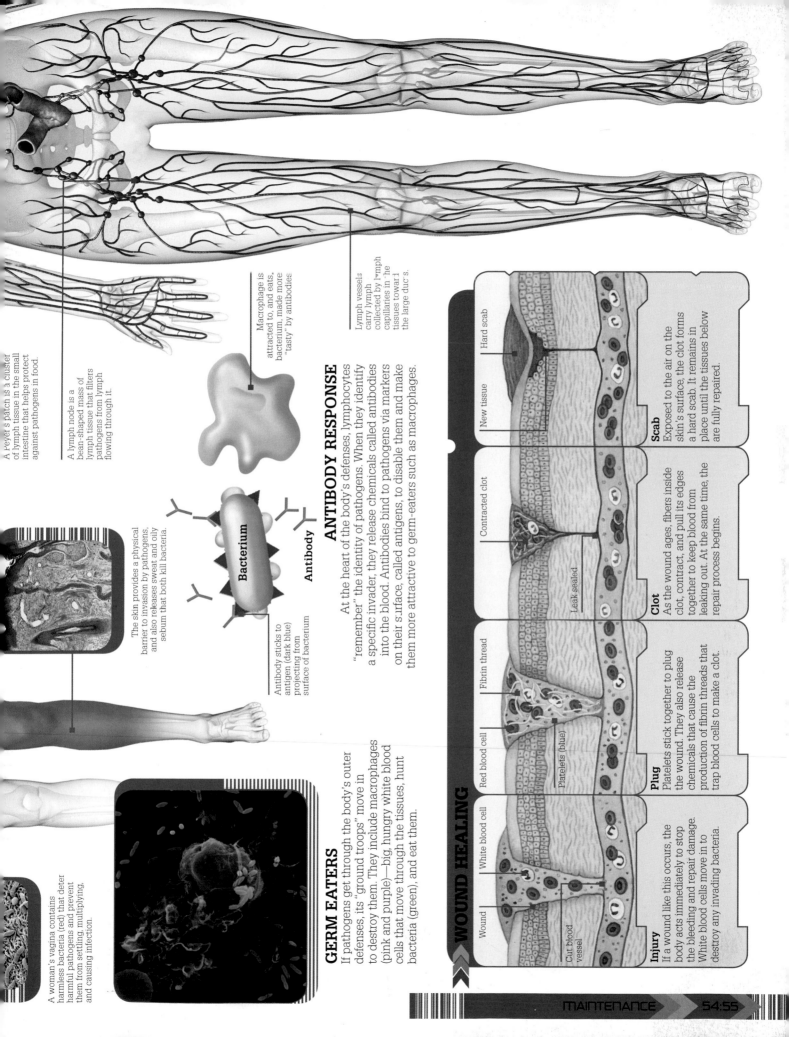

A Peyer's patch is a cluster of lymph tissue in the small intestine that helps protect against pathogens in food.

A lymph node is a bean-shaped mass of lymph tissue that filters pathogens from lymph flowing through it.

Macrophage is attracted to, and eats, bacterium, made more "tasty" by antibodies

Lymph vessels carry lymph collected by lymph capillaries in the tissues toward the large ducts.

The skin provides a physical barrier to invasion by pathogens, and also releases sweat and oily sebum that both kill bacteria.

A woman's vagina contains harmless bacteria (red) that deter harmful pathogens and prevent them from settling, multiplying, and causing infection.

Antibody sticks to antigen (dark blue) projecting from surface of bacterium

Bacterium

Antibody

ANTIBODY RESPONSE

At the heart of the body's defenses, lymphocytes "remember" the identity of pathogens. When they identify a specific invader, they release chemicals called antibodies into the blood. Antibodies bind to pathogens via markers on their surface, called antigens, to disable them and make them more attractive to germ-eaters such as macrophages.

GERM EATERS

If pathogens get through the body's outer defenses, its "ground troops" move in to destroy them. They include macrophages (pink and purple)—big, hungry white blood cells that move through the tissues, hunt bacteria (green), and eat them.

▶▶ WOUND HEALING

| White blood cell | Wound | Red blood cell | Fibrin thread | Contracted clot | New tissue | Hard scab |

Cut blood vessel · Platelets (blue) · Leak sealed

Injury
If a wound like this occurs, the body acts immediately to stop the bleeding and repair damage. White blood cells move in to destroy any invading bacteria.

Plug
Platelets stick together to plug the wound. They also release chemicals that cause the production of fibrin threads that trap blood cells to make a clot.

Clot
As the wound ages, fibers inside clot, contract, and pull its edges together to keep blood from leaking out. At the same time, the repair process begins.

Scab
Exposed to the air on the skin's surface, the clot forms a hard scab. It remains in place until the tissues below are fully repaired.

Getting oxygen

Although the body can cope without food or water for some time, it must have an uninterrupted supply of oxygen. Oxygen is needed by body cells to release energy, which generates carbon dioxide as waste. The body gets its oxygen, and disposes of carbon dioxide, by breathing air into and out of the respiratory system.

BRONCHIAL TREE

The mass of passages that carry air into and out of the lungs resembles an upside-down tree, as shown by this resin cast. In this "bronchial tree," the trachea forms the trunk, the bronchi are branches, and the bronchioles are twigs.

Hairlike cilia beat to move mucus

The nasal cavity warms, moistens, and cleans breathed-in air. It is covered with sticky mucus, which traps dirt and pathogens and is moved by cilia to the throat.

Trachea

Mass of bronchi branch from primary bronchi and divide into smaller bronchioles

Left primary bronchus supplies left lung

The trachea, the main airway, carries air between the throat and the lungs and is reinforced by C-shaped rings of cartilage that prevent its collapse during breathing.

The trachea lining is covered with mucus that traps any fine particles not filtered out by the nasal cavity. Its cilia (green) move contaminated mucus to the throat.

The right lung is slightly larger than the left lung and is concealed by the rib cage, which both protects it and plays a key part in breathing.

The ribs that curve forward from the backbone, together with the intercostal muscles that link them, form the wall of the chest that encloses the two lungs.

RESPIRATORY SYSTEM

This system consists of the two lungs and the airways that carry air in and out of the body. The nasal cavity cleans incoming air, trapping particles and pathogens that might damage the lungs. This process continues as air passes down the trachea before entering the bronchi that carry air into each lung. These bronchi divide repeatedly, finally ending in the alveoli, through which oxygen enters the bloodstream.

The diaphragm is a sheet of muscle immediately below the lungs. It separates the chest from the abdominal cavity and plays a major role in breathing.

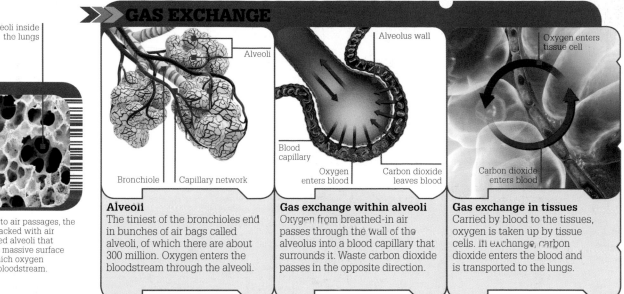

Alveolus wall

Oxygen enters tissue cell

Alveoli

Blood capillary

Oxygen enters blood

Carbon dioxide leaves blood

Carbon dioxide enters blood

Oxygen enters tissue cell

Bronchiole | Capillary network

Alveoli
The tiniest of the bronchioles end in bunches of air bags called alveoli, of which there are about 300 million. Oxygen enters the bloodstream through the alveoli.

Gas exchange within alveoli
Oxygen from breathed-in air passes through the wall of the alveolus into a blood capillary that surrounds it. Waste carbon dioxide passes in the opposite direction.

Gas exchange in tissues
Carried by blood to the tissues, oxygen is taken up by tissue cells. In exchange, carbon dioxide enters the blood and is transported to the lungs.

Alveoli inside the lungs

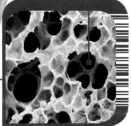

In addition to air passages, the lungs are packed with air spaces called alveoli that provide the massive surface through which oxygen enters the bloodstream.

Together, the alveoli provide a surface area of around 753 square feet (70 square meters), the floor area of a two bedroom apartment.

Two lungs fill most of chest cavity

One of the main bronchi in the left lung. It divides into smaller bronchi, which branch into even smaller tubes called bronchioles.

Heart

Aorta

Backbone

The heart pumps oxygen-poor blood to the lungs to pick up oxygen, then pumps the resulting oxygen-enriched blood to the tissues, where it is in constant demand.

The left lung is smaller than the right lung and has a "notch" on its inner surface to make room for the heart, which is tilted toward the left side of the body.

Pleural membranes covering the lungs and lining the chest slide over each other during breathing so that the lungs can expand and deflate easily.

LUNGS AND HEART
This CT scan through the chest shows the close proximity of the lungs to the heart. This means that blood has only a short distance to travel from the heart to pick up oxygen before being pumped to the rest of the body.

Breathing air

To replace the oxygen that is used up by body cells, and remove the carbon dioxide waste those cells generate, the air in the lungs is constantly renewed by breathing, or ventilation. Breathing movements are made by the diaphragm and rib muscles. They alter the chest size to move air in or out of the lungs.

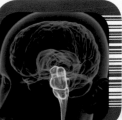

The breathing rate is controlled by respiratory centers in the brain stem (orange) at the base of the brain (green).

Neck muscles aid inhalation during forced breathing by pulling the rib cage upward to further increase the volume of the chest cavity.

External intercostal muscles, which run from rib to rib, contract to pull the rib cage upward and outward. This movement is followed by the lungs.

Epiglottis closes entrance to larynx during swallowing

Arytenoid cartilage anchors vocal cords

Hyoid bone anchors neck muscles that move larynx during speech

Cricoid cartilage attaches larynx to trachea

Thyroid cartilage forms "Adam's apple"

Vocal cords stretch from front to back of larynx

C-shaped cartilage rings reinforce trachea

As the lungs passively follow the expansion of the chest cavity, they fill with air brought in from the outside along the airways.

LARYNX
Also called the voice box, the larynx connects the throat to the trachea and produces sounds. It is built from a framework of cartilage plates including the epiglottis and the thyroid, cricoid, and arytenoid cartilages.

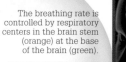

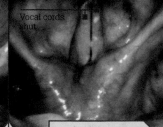

MAKING SOUNDS

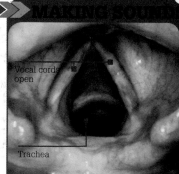

Vocal cords open

Trachea

Vocal cords shut

Inhalation (breathing in)

The diaphragm, a dome-shaped sheet of muscle that separates the chest from the abdomen, contracts and flattens to stretch lungs downward.

Vocal cords open
The vocal cords produce sounds. During normal breathing, as this endoscope view down the throat shows, they are pulled wide apart to allow air to pass through.

Vocal cords closed
If air is forced between closed vocal cords, they vibrate and make sounds. Those sounds are shaped into understandable speech by the tongue, cheeks, and lips.

VENTILATION

The lungs cannot move on their own; they follow changes in the volume of the chest. During inhalation, the diaphragm and external intercostal muscles increase this volume. The lungs follow, sucking in air as they expand to fill the space. During exhalation, the diaphragm and external intercostal muscles relax, the volume decreases, and air is squeezed from the lungs. During forced breathing (exercise), other muscles enhance chest movements.

PREVENTING CHOKING

When we swallow food or water, breathing stops temporarily. The epiglottis, the flap at the front of the larynx, covers the entrance to the larynx to prevent food from getting in, blocking the airway, and causing choking. If this happens, coughing automatically attempts to force the object into the throat.

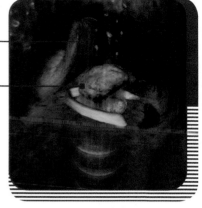

Epiglottis

Food entering airway

The trachea is held open by cartilage rings to prevent it from collapsing when air passes through it during breathing.

The lungs deflate as the space inside the chest cavity decreases, and air is squeezed out of them through the airways to the outside.

The internal intercostal muscles pull the ribs downward and inward during forced breathing to aid the action of the diaphragm.

At rest, we breathe in and out between 12 and 15 times every minute. During exercise, this rate can more than double.

REFLEX MOVEMENTS

In addition to normal breathing, there are other reflex breathing movements. Coughing, for example, automatically clears any irritation or blockage from the trachea. After air pressure builds up behind closed vocal cords, they open to release a blast of air through the mouth. Sneezing works in a similar way to clear the nose. Other reflex breathing movements include yawning and hiccups.

The diaphragm relaxes and is pushed up into a dome shape by pressure from the abdominal organs beneath it, thereby decreasing space inside the chest.

Exhalation (breathing out)

The abdominal muscles play a part in forced breathing by helping to pull the rib cage downward to further decrease the volume inside the chest.

Eating and drinking

Without food, the body would be unable to grow, repair, or maintain itself, or obtain energy. All foods, however delicious, are useless to the body until they have been chopped and digested to release nutrients that can be used by body cells. The first part of that process happens in the mouth.

The hard palate forms the roof of the mouth against which food is pushed prior to swallowing.

DENTAL TOOL KIT

The mouth contains a dental tool kit of different types of teeth that together convert food into pieces small enough to be swallowed. Incisors cut and slice, canines grip and pierce, and premolars chew and grind—a process completed by the larger molars.

Canine

Molar

Incisor

Premolar

The tongue is a muscular, flexible organ that moves between the teeth during chewing.

Enamel crown

Bony dentine shapes tooth

This cross section of a tooth shows the hard enamel crown, dentine, the pulp cavity (which contains nerves and blood vessels), and the root.

Pulp cavity

Root anchors tooth in jaw

TOOTH DECAY

This microscopic view of a tooth shows a layer of plaque (yellow) on its surface. Plaque is a sticky mixture of food remains and mouth bacteria that stays glued to the tooth's surface unless teeth are brushed regularly. As they feed on leftovers, bacteria release acids that excavate holes in tooth enamel and dentine. Left untreated, this causes painful tooth decay, a disease that destroys living pulp tissues.

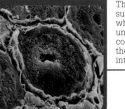

The submaxillary and submandibular glands, which release saliva under the tongue, consist of acini such as these that secrete saliva into a central duct.

The epiglottis closes the entrance to the larynx during swallowing.

We have two sets of teeth during our lifetime: 20 baby (deciduous) teeth as children and 32 permanent adult teeth (16 in each jaw).

MOUTH AND THROAT

The mouth is the first part of the digestive system—the place where food is converted into a form that can be swallowed. Having been bitten off by the front teeth, food is chewed into small particles and mixed by the tongue with watery, slimy saliva that gushes into the mouth from three pairs of salivary glands. Once chewing is completed, the tongue pushes food toward the throat so it can be swallowed.

Saliva released by this parotid gland lubricates food and contains an enzyme that digests starch.

BALANCED DIET

A balanced diet consists of a variety of different, preferably fresh, foods that provide essential nutrients, such as carbohydrates and proteins, in the right amounts to keep us healthy. This chart shows the proportions of food types we should eat daily.

Regular exercise, combined with a balanced diet, is vitally important in keeping your weight within the range that is best for your health.

Grains
These foods, including bread and wheat, are rich in complex carbohydrates such as starch, which is digested into glucose, the body's main source of energy.

Vegetables
Broccoli, peppers, carrots, and other vegetables are very good sources of vitamins and minerals—nutrients that are essential for health, but are needed only in tiny amounts.

Fruits
Apples, oranges, and other fruits provide plenty of vitamins and, like vegetables, are good sources of dietary fiber, which makes digestion more efficient.

Oils
Oils are very energy-rich and should be eaten in small amounts. Junk foods that are full of oils, fats, salt, and sugar should only form a small part of a balanced diet.

Dairy
Some dairy products, such as butter, are high in animal fat, and should be eaten only in small amounts. Others, such as milk, are good sources of protein and the mineral calcium.

Meat and beans
Along with fish, poultry, eggs, and nuts, meat and beans provide us with proteins—the nutrients that supply the raw materials for growth and repair.

The throat (pharynx) connects the mouth to the opening of the esophagus.

The esophagus is normally flattened unless food is passing down it to the stomach.

Trachea (windpipe)

FROM MOUTH TO STOMACH

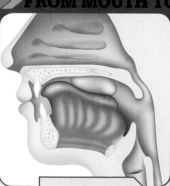

Mouth
Swallowing moves food from the mouth to the stomach and is a three-stage process. In the mouth, the tongue pushes a food bolus (ball) toward the throat.

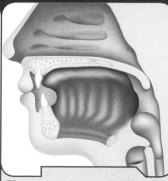

Throat
Food touching the throat triggers a reflex. The epiglottis blocks the entrance to the larynx, to prevent choking, while muscle contractions push food to the esophagus.

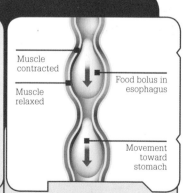

Muscle contracted

Muscle relaxed

Food bolus in esophagus

Movement toward stomach

Esophagus
Finally, peristalsis (waves of contraction of smooth muscle in the wall of the esophagus) pushes food toward the stomach. The journey takes around 10 seconds.

Food processor

The food we eat is processed by the digestive system. It uses two mechanisms to digest food into simple nutrients that can be used by body cells. Mechanical digestion, such as the churning of food by the stomach, breaks food into small particles. Chemical digestion by enzymes converts large food molecules into smaller ones.

The liver processes nutrients once they are absorbed by the body. It also stores some nutrients (including glucose), produces bile, and removes harmful substances from blood.

The gall bladder is a stretchy bag that collects and concentrates bile made by the liver before releasing it into the small intestine.

CHEMICAL DIGESTERS

Fat molecules   Fatty acid

Lipase

Monoglyceride—fatty acid joined to glycerol

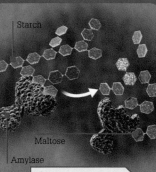

Starch

Maltose

Amylase

Peptide

Protein

Protease

Fat breakdown
Some enzymes are released into the duodenum in pancreatic juice. The enzyme lipase breaks down fat molecules into fatty acids and monoglycerides.

Carbohydrate breakdown
The enzyme amylase breaks down carbohydrate starch into a sugar called maltose. Intestine enzymes later break down maltose into glucose, which the body absorbs.

Protein breakdown
The enzyme protease breaks down protein into shorter units called peptides. Like all enzymes, protease is unchanged during the process, ready to be used again.

STOMACH

Swallow the food

1 When food reaches the stomach, gastric glands (left) in the stomach's lining release acidic gastric juice that contains pepsin, a protein-digesting enzyme. Contraction of the stomach's muscular wall churns food and gastric juice into a creamy liquid that is squirted into the duodenum.

The appendix is a fingerlike extension of the cecum that stores useful bacteria.

GALL BLADDER AND PANCREAS
Fluids from the gall bladder and pancreas empty through ducts into the duodenum to jump-start digestion in the small intestine. The gall bladder releases bile that converts fats into tiny, easy-to-digest droplets. Pancreatic juice contains enzymes that digest carbohydrates, proteins, and fats.

Gall bladder

Duct carries bile from liver to gall bladder

Common bile duct to duodenum from gall bladder

Pancreatic duct empties into duodenum

Pancreas

Duodenum— first section of small intestine

The cecum is the short, pouchlike first section of the large intestine.

The colon, the main part of the large intestine, extends from cecum to rectum and carries waste material from the small intestine, removing water from it to form feces.

The esophagus connects the throat to the stomach and pushes chewed food toward the stomach by peristalsis—waves of contraction of its muscular wall.

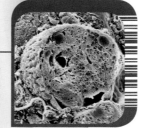

Acinar cells of the pancreas secrete enzyme-containing pancreatic juice that empties into the small intestine and digests various food molecules.

The stomach is an elastic, muscular bag that partially digests and stores food before releasing it into the duodenum, the first part of the small intestine.

The small intestine is the longest part of the GI tract where most digestion and absorption occurs.

Trillions of bacteria (pink) in the colon digest waste. This releases useful substances such as vitamin K that are absorbed and used by the body.

The rectum is the last part of the large intestine, which stores feces ready for disposal.

The anus is the lower opening of the GI tract, through which feces are pushed out.

SMALL INTESTINE

2 Millions of these microscopic villi line the small intestine. They carry enzymes that complete the digestion of carbohydrates, proteins, and fats that started with pancreatic enzymes. The resulting nutrients, such as glucose and amino acids, are absorbed via villi into the bloodstream.

Break down the food

COLON

3 This endoscopic view shows the inside of the colon, glistening with slimy, lubricating mucus. The longest part of the large intestine, the colon, moves undigested waste toward the rectum, while absorbing water from the waste to create semisolid feces.

Release the waste

DIGESTIVE SYSTEM

The gastrointestinal (GI) tract, the core of the digestive system, is a long tube that extends from the mouth to the anus. Each part of the GI tract—the mouth, throat, esophagus, stomach, small intestine, and large intestine—has its own role in the digestive process. In addition, the teeth, tongue, salivary glands, gall bladder, liver, and pancreas are organs attached to the GI tract that aid digestion.

In addition to undigested food and dead cells, feces contain millions of bacteria. That's why you need to wash your hands after going to the bathroom.

Liver at work

This big, dark red organ plays a vital part in maintaining the constant conditions inside the body that keep it working efficiently. As blood flows through the liver, its cells work tirelessly to process the products of digestion, remove poisons and debris, break down hormones, and make bile.

The branch of the hepatic vein that collects blood processed by liver cells and empties it into the inferior vena cava.

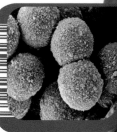

Hepatocytes, or liver cells, such as these make up the liver and carry out its hundreds of functions including the processing of nutrients.

INSIDE THE LIVER

The liver is made up of sesame seed–sized processing plants called lobules. Each lobule is made up of sheets of liver cells that process blood as it flows between them, storing some substances, breaking down others, and releasing some for use by the body.

NUTRIENTS AND THE LIVER

Following digestion, simple nutrients (glucose, fatty acids, and amino acids) are transported from the small intestine to the liver. Here, they are processed to adjust the level of each nutrient in the blood before being dispatched to, and used by, every body cell.

GLUCOSE
The major energy source for body cells, glucose is the product of carbohydrate breakdown during digestion.

FATTY ACIDS
The result of fat digestion, fatty acids are used to make cell membranes or stored as energy-rich fats.

AMINO ACIDS
These are the building blocks used by all cells to make the proteins needed for cell building, repair, division, and metabolism.

The gall bladder, behind the liver, receives bile produced by liver cells through a bile duct and stores it.

All cells, including this brain cell, need energy. Glucose is the main source, but some cells use fatty acids. Amino acids are a last resort.

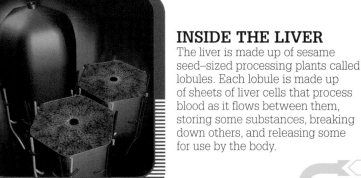

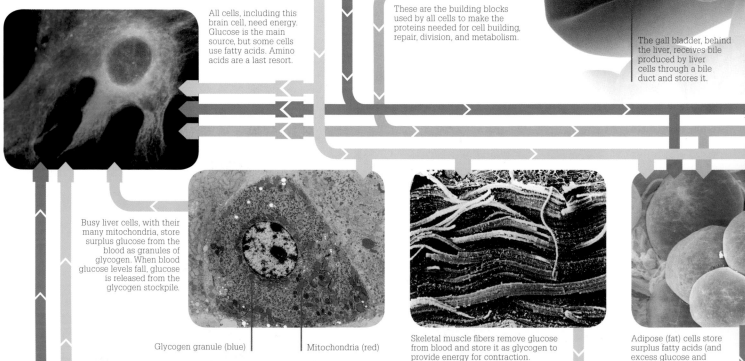

Busy liver cells, with their many mitochondria, store surplus glucose from the blood as granules of glycogen. When blood glucose levels fall, glucose is released from the glycogen stockpile.

Glycogen granule (blue)   Mitochondria (red)

Skeletal muscle fibers remove glucose from blood and store it as glycogen to provide energy for contraction.

Adipose (fat) cells store surplus fatty acids (and excess glucose and amino acids) as fat.

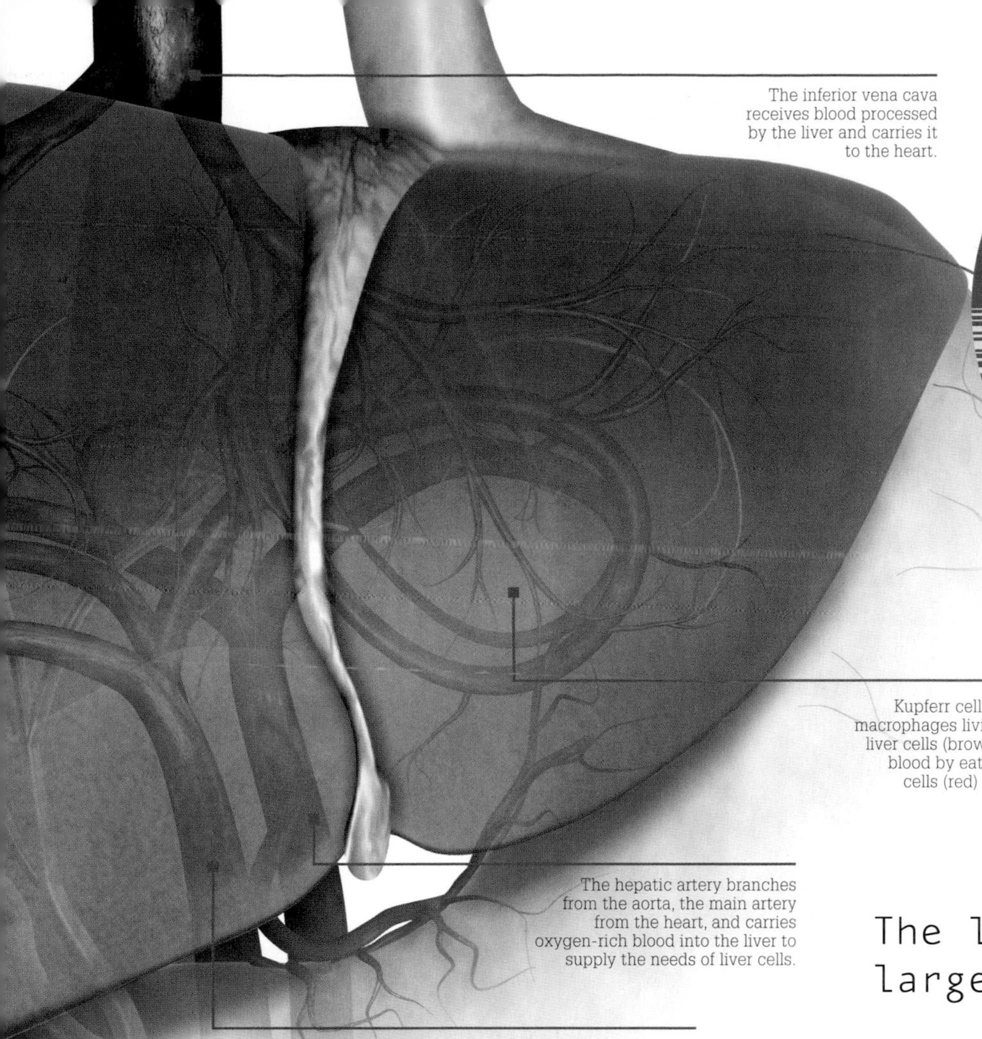

The inferior vena cava receives blood processed by the liver and carries it to the heart.

CHEMICAL FACTORY

Inside the liver, many chemical reactions occur within cells to perform more than 500 functions. Unusually, the liver receives blood from two sources—the heart and intestines—and the cells work on this blood. Among other things, they either store, break down, or dispatch glucose, fatty acids, amino acids, minerals, and vitamins received from the small intestine. The only direct digestive function liver cells have is to make bile.

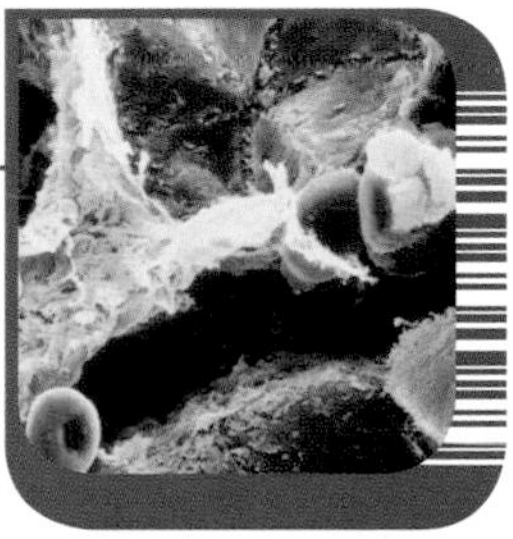

Kupferr cells (yellow) are macrophages living alongside liver cells (brown) that clean blood by eating old blood cells (red) and bacteria.

The hepatic artery branches from the aorta, the main artery from the heart, and carries oxygen-rich blood into the liver to supply the needs of liver cells.

The liver is the body's largest internal organ.

The hepatic portal vein carries oxygen-poor but nutrient-rich blood from the small intestine and other parts of the gastrointestinal (GI) tract and delivers it to liver cells for processing.

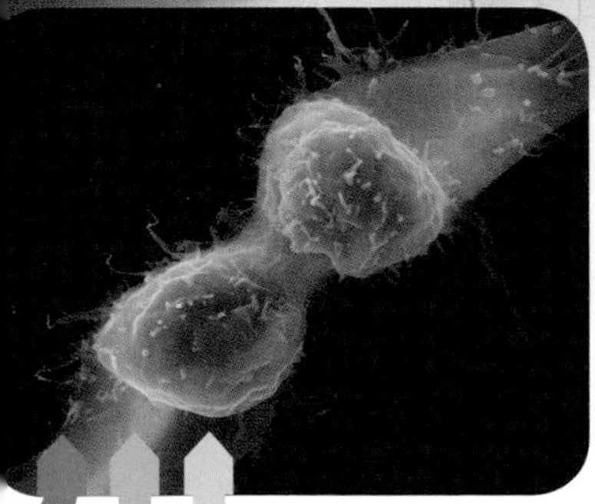

Cells divide to enable growth and repair. Glucose and fatty acids provide the energy for cell division, while amino acids help construct the two new cells.

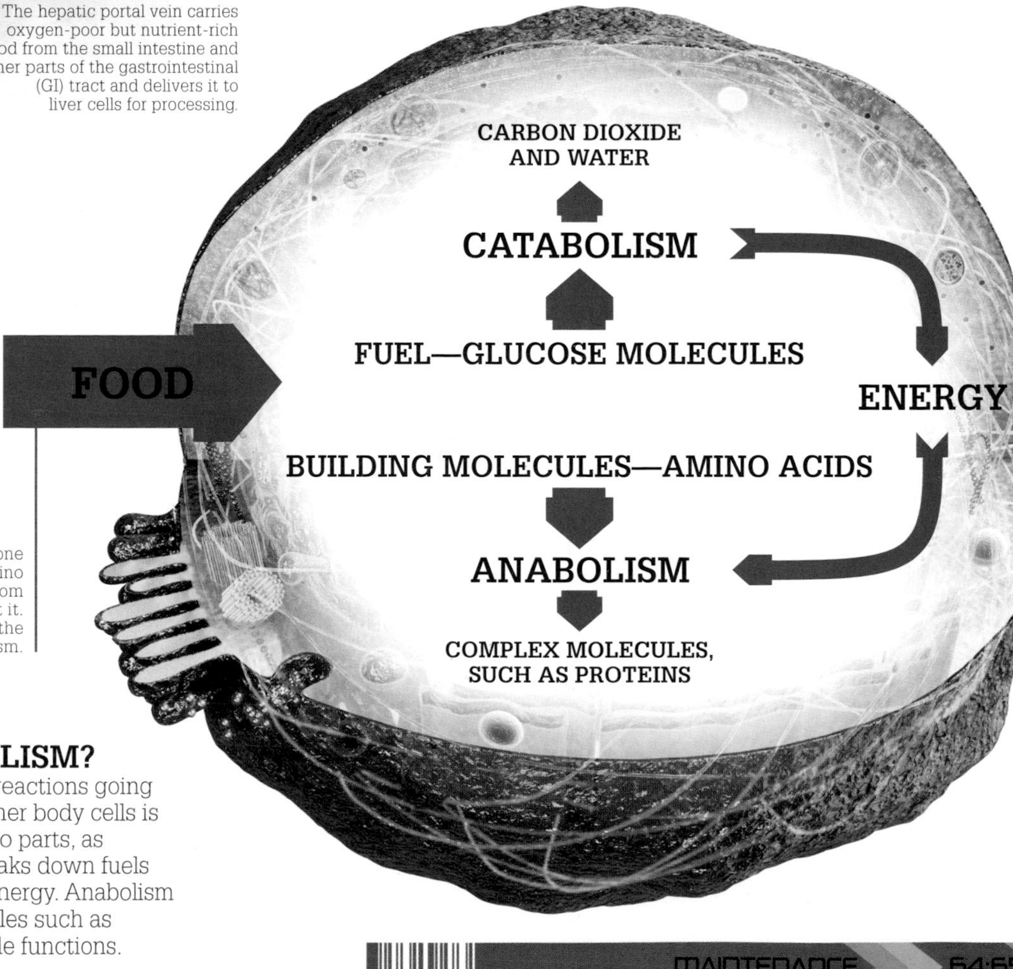

A cell such as this one receives glucose, amino acids, and fatty acids from the blood flowing past it. These nutrients provide the raw materials for metabolism.

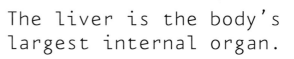

CARBON DIOXIDE AND WATER

CATABOLISM

FUEL—GLUCOSE MOLECULES

FOOD

ENERGY

BUILDING MOLECULES—AMINO ACIDS

ANABOLISM

COMPLEX MOLECULES, SUCH AS PROTEINS

WHAT IS METABOLISM?

The thousands of chemical reactions going on inside the liver and all other body cells is called metabolism. It has two parts, as shown here. Catabolism breaks down fuels such as glucose to release energy. Anabolism uses energy to build molecules such as proteins, which have multiple functions.

Waste removal

As blood flows around the body, it picks up cells' waste products as well as water and salts that have been consumed in food and drinks. In order to keep blood concentration constant, the kidneys, part of the urinary system, remove waste and excess water and salts. The resulting watery urine is then expelled from the body.

Daily, around 40 gallons (180 liters) of fluid is filtered from the blood by kidney nephrons, but only 3 pints (1.5 liters) of waste leaves the body as urine.

URINARY SYSTEM

Two kidneys, two ureters, the bladder, and the urethra make up the urinary system. Set high on the back wall of the abdomen, the energy-hungry kidneys—they consume 25 percent of the body's energy—process blood to make urine. Carried from the kidneys by ureters, urine is stored in the bladder until the time is right to release it through the urethra.

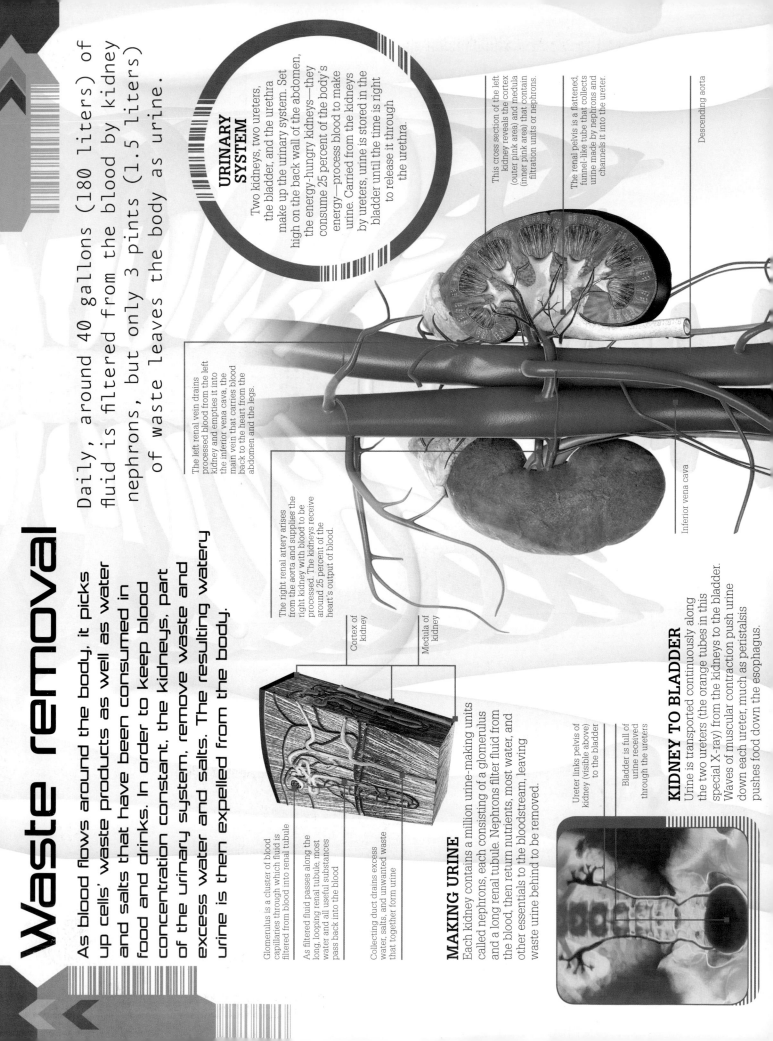

The left renal vein drains processed blood from the left kidney and empties it into the inferior vena cava, the main vein that carries blood back to the heart from the abdomen and the legs.

The right renal artery arises from the aorta and supplies the right kidney with blood to be processed. The kidneys receive around 25 percent of the heart's output of blood.

This cross section of the left kidney reveals the cortex (outer pink area) and medula (inner pink area) that contain filtration units or nephrons.

The renal pelvis is a flattened, funnel-like tube that collects urine made by nephrons and channels it into the ureter.

Descending aorta

Inferior vena cava

Cortex of kidney

Medula of kidney

MAKING URINE

Each kidney contains a million urine-making units called nephrons, each consisting of a glomerulus and a long renal tubule. Nephrons filter fluid from the blood, then return nutrients, most water, and other essentials to the bloodstream, leaving waste urine behind to be removed.

Glomerulus is a cluster of blood capillaries through which fluid is filtered from blood into renal tubule

As filtered fluid passes along the long, looping renal tubule, most water and all useful substances pass back into the blood

Collecting duct drains excess water, salts, and unwanted waste that together form urine

Ureter links pelvis of kidney (visible above) to the bladder

Bladder is full of urine received through the ureters

KIDNEY TO BLADDER

Urine is transported continuously along the two ureters (the orange tubes in this special X-ray) from the kidneys to the bladder. Waves of muscular contraction push urine down each ureter, much as peristalsis pushes food down the esophagus.

MALE SYSTEM

The male urinary system is similar to the female version, except for the urethra. After leaving the bladder, the male urethra immediately passes through the prostate gland. In addition, it is longer than the female's, and extends to the tip of the penis.

Hypothalamus (yellow) is a small but important part of the brain

Prostate gland is part of reproductive system

Urethra runs along the length of the penis

The right ureter maintains a one-way flow of urine from the right kidney to the bladder.

The bladder is a stretchy, muscular bag that stores urine and releases it when a sphincter guarding the exit to the urethra is released.

The urethra is the tube that carries the urine outside the body during urination.

FEELING THIRSTY

One of the many jobs of the hypothalamus is to control thirst. Its thirst center monitors the concentration of the blood. If blood is too concentrated and doesn't contain enough water, the thirst center creates a feeling of thirst so a person feels the need to drink.

FILLING AND EMPTYING

Filling bladder
As the bladder (green in this X-ray) fills with urine, stretch receptors in its wall send messages to the brain. Only then does a person feel the need to urinate.

Emptying bladder
Under conscious control, a sphincter muscle at the base of the bladder relaxes, and the bladder's wall squeezes urine out through the urethra.

TESTING URINE

About 95 percent of urine is water; the rest is dissolved substances such as waste urea. Doctors test for abnormal levels of certain substances in urine to help them diagnose diseases. A dipstick is dipped into a urine sample (below) to detect the levels of specific substances.

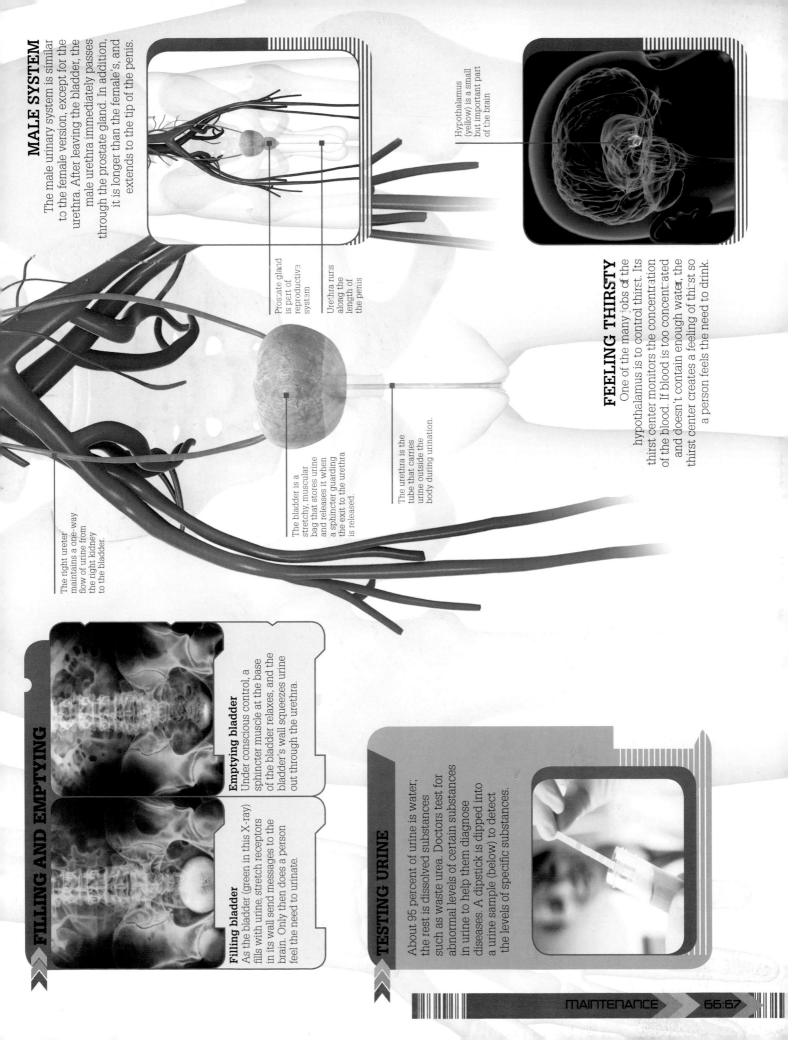

Glossary

Abdomen
The lower part of the trunk between the chest and the pelvis that contains most of the digestive organs.

Amino acid
One of a group of 20 substances that are the building blocks of proteins.

Antibody
A type of protein released by immune-system cells that binds to pathogens and marks them for destruction.

Antigen
A marker on the surface of pathogens that is recognized as "foreign" by the immune system; also a marker on red blood cells that determines blood types.

Association neuron
A type of nerve cell, found in the central nervous system, that relays nerve impulses from one neuron to another.

Autonomic nervous system (ANS)
The part of the nervous system that controls unconscious functions such as heart rate and pupil diameter.

Axon
Also called a nerve fiber, the long filament that carries nerve impulses away from a neuron's cell body towards another neuron or muscle fiber.

Bacteria
A group of microorganisms, a few of which cause disease in humans.

Base
One of four substances—adenine, cytosine, guanine, and thymine—that provide the "letters" of the coded instructions in DNA molecules.

Billion
A number equal to one thousand million (1,000,000,000).

Calcium
A type of mineral used by the body in muscle contraction and to build bones and teeth.

Carbohydrate
One of a group of substances, including sugars such as glucose, and complex carbohydrates such as glycogen, that provide the body's main energy supply.

Cartilage
A tough, flexible type of connective tissue that helps support the body and covers the ends of bones in joints.

Cell
One of the trillions of microscopic living units from which the body is constructed.

Cellular respiration
The process by which energy is released from glucose and other fuels inside cells.

Central nervous system (CNS)
The controlling part of the nervous system that consists of the brain and spinal cord.

Chromosome
One of 46 threadlike packages of DNA found in the nucleus of every body cell.

CT (Computed Tomography) scan
An imaging technique that uses X-rays and a computer to produce 2-D and 3-D images of body organs.

DNA (Deoxyribonucleic Acid)
One of the long molecules found inside the nucleus that contain the instructions to build and run a cell.

Endocrine gland
A type of gland, such as the pituitary gland, that releases hormones.

Endoscope
A viewing instrument introduced through an opening, such as the mouth, in order to look inside the body.

Energy
The capacity to perform work, essential to maintaining life.

Enzyme
A type of protein that greatly speeds up the rate of chemical reactions both inside cells and during the digestion of food by the digestive system.

Fat
A type of substance found in food that is used as an energy store in adipose (fat) tissue in the body.

Fatty acid
One of the building blocks of fats.

Feedback
A control mechanism that, for example, regulates levels of hormones in the bloodstream.

Fertilization
The joining together of sperm (male sex cell) and egg (female sex cell).

Gene
One of the 23,000 instructions, each a section of a DNA molecule, needed to build a body and which are passed on to offspring.

Germ
The common name for a pathogen.

Gland
A collection of cells that secrete a substance inside or onto the body.

Glucose
A sugar carried in the bloodstream that is the main source of energy for body cells.

Hepatic
A term used to describe something relating to the liver.

Hormone
A substance released into the bloodstream by an endocrine gland. It controls body activities by altering the activities of target cells.

Hypothalamus
A small structure located in the base of the brain that controls many body activities, including thirst and body temperature, and which links the nervous and endocrine systems.

Imaging technique
A form of technology, such as a CT scan or X-ray, that is used by doctors to create a "picture" of the inside of a living body.

Immune system
The body's major defense mechanism that consists primarily of white blood cells in the blood and lymph systems that destroy pathogens.

Joint
A part of the skeleton where two or more bones meet.

Keratin
A tough, waterproof protein that fills the cells that make up hairs, nails, and the upper epidermis.

Ligament
A tough connective tissue that holds bones together where they meet at joints.

Lymph
Excess fluid that is drained from the tissues by lymph vessels and returned to the bloodstream.

Lymphocyte
A type of white blood cell that plays a key role in the immune system, including releasing antibodies.

Macrophage
A type of white blood cell that engulfs and destroys pathogens and has an important role in the immune system.

Metabolism
A term used to describe all the chemical reactions going on inside the body, especially within cells.

Mineral
One of about 20 substances, including calcium and iron, that should be present in the diet.

Mitochondrion (plural: Mitochondria)
An organelle found in the cell's cytoplasm that releases energy.

Mitosis
A type of cell division that produces two identical offspring cells.

Motor neuron
A type of neuron, found in nerves, that carries nerve impulses from the CNS to the muscles.

MRA (Magnetic Resonance Angiography) scan
An imaging technique that uses magnetism, radio waves, and a computer to create pictures of body organs and tissues.

Muscle fiber
A muscle cell.

Nerve impulse
A tiny electrical signal that is transmitted along a neuron at high speed.

Neuron
One of billions of nerve cells that makes up the nervous system.

Organ
A body part, such as the stomach or kidney, that has a specific role or roles and is made up of two or more tissues.

Organelle
A tiny structure inside a cell, such as a mitochondrion, that has a specific function.

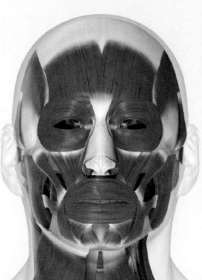

Oxygen
A gas found in air that is used by body cells to release energy from glucose during cellular respiration.

Pathogen
A type of microorganism, such as a bacterium or virus, that causes disease in humans.

Peristalsis
The wave of muscular contractions in the wall of a hollow organ that, for example, pushes food down the esophagus.

PET (Positron Emission Tomography) scan
An imaging technique that uses radioactive substances injected into the body to reveal activity levels in body organs such as the brain.

Protein
One of a group of substances, the most diverse in the body. Proteins perform many roles, including that of enzymes, antibodies, and parts of cell membranes.

Radionuclide scan
An imaging technique that uses radioactive substances to show the functioning of bones and some other organs.

Reflex action
A rapid, automatic response that is carried out without our being aware of it, and which often protects the body from harm.

Renal
A term used to describe something relating to the kidney.

Sensory neuron
A type of neuron, found in nerves, that carries nerve impulses from the sensory receptors to the CNS.

Sensory receptor
A specialized nerve cell or the end of a sensory neuron that detects a stimulus, such as light or sound.

Sex chromosome
One of two chromosomes in the nucleus of each body cell that determine whether a person is male or female.

Sphincter
A ring of muscle around a passageway or opening that opens and closes to control the flow of material, such as urine or food, through it.

Spinal nerve
One of 31 pairs of nerves that arise from the spinal cord.

Synapse
The junction between two neurons in which they are separated by a tiny gap.

Tendon
A cord of tough, connective tissue that links muscle to bone.

Tissue
A group of cells of the same or similar type that work together to perform a particular function.

Trillion
A number equal to one million million (1,000,000,000,000).

Ultrasound
An imaging technique that uses inaudible, high-frequency sound waves to produce pictures of a developing fetus or of body tissues.

Virus
An infectious chemical package that multiplies inside human cells and causes diseases such as the common cold and flu.

Vitamin
One of a number of substances, including vitamins A and C, needed in small amounts in the diet to maintain health.

X-ray
An imaging technique that uses a form of radiation to reveal bones.

Index

Credits

Dorling Kindersley would like to thank Clare Gray for proofreading and Jackie Brind for the index.

The publisher would like to thank the following for their kind permission to reproduce their photographs:
(**Key:** a-above; b-below/bottom; c-center; f-far; l-left; r-right; t-top)

4 Corbis: Clouds Hill Imaging Ltd. (tr); **5 Corbis:** Dennis Kunkel Microscopy, Inc./Visuals Unlimited (tl); **Corbis:** Dr. Richard Kessel & Dr. Randy K/Visuals Unlimited (tr); **6–7 Corbis:** Clouds Hill Imaging Ltd.; **8–9 Science Photo Library (SPL):** Simon Fraser; **8 SPL:** Scientifica, Visuals Unlimited (tl) **Getty Images:** Garry Hunter (tr); **SPL:** David M. Martin, MD (bc); **SPL:** Alain Pol, ISM (br); **9 SPL:** Pasieka (tl); **SPL:** Sovereign, ISM (tc); **SPL:** Scott Camazine (bl); **10 Corbis:** Dennis Kunkel Microscopy, Inc./Visuals Unlimited (ca); **Getty Images:** Brand X Pictures/Steve Allen (cl); **SPL:** Steve Gschmeissner (bl); **SPL:** Eye Of Science (fbl); **Getty Images:** Steve Gschmeissner/SPL (br); **SPL:** David McCarthy (br); **11 Corbis:** Steve Gschmeissner/Science Photo Library (tr); **SPL:** Professors P. Motta & T. Naguro (cr); **SPL:** Professors P. Motta & T. Naguro (bl); **12 SPL:** CNRI (cl); **13 Getty Images:** Photodisc (tl); **SPL:** Kenneth Eward/BioGrafx (cl); **SPL:** Steve Gschmeissner (crb); **14 SPL:** Susumu Nishinaga (bl); **15 SPL:** Professors P. M. Motta & J. Van Blerkom (c); **SPL:** Zephyr (cra); **Corbis:** David P. Hall (crb); **SPL:** Professor P. M. Motta/University "La Sapienza", Rome (bl); **16 Getty Images:** Wehr (cl); **SPL:** Professors P. M. Motta, K. R. Porter & P. M. Andrews (c); **17 Corbis:** Ole Graf (ca); **SPL:** Power and Syred (cr); **19 SPL:** Anatomical Travelogue (br); **20 Corbis:** David Scharf/Science Faction (fcl); **SPL:** Simon Fraser; Paul Gunning (cl); **SPL:** Steve Gschmeissner (cra); **Corbis:** Photo Quest Ltd/Science Photo Library (br); **Dorling Kindersley:** NASA (cr); **21 SPL:** Power and Syred (tl); **SPL:** Steve Gschmeissner (cb); **Corbis:** ImageShop (bl); **SPL:** Institut Paoli-Calmettes, ISM (br); **22 Getty Images:** Mike Kemp (bl); **23 Getty Images:** Pasieka/SPL (tr); **SPL:** Dept. Of Clinical Radiology, Salisbury District Hospital (cb); **Corbis:** Ted Horowitz (br); **24 SPL:** Professor P. M. Motta/University "La Sapienza", Rome (tr); **Corbis:** Thom Lang (bl); **25 Corbis:** Koji Aoki/Aflo (tr); **SPL:** Steve Gschmeissner (cr); **SPL:** Steve Gschmeissner (cra); **SPL:** Ted Kinsman (br); **26 SPL:** Don W. Fawcett (br); **27 SPL:** Steve Gschmeissner (bc); **28–29 Corbis:** Dennis Kunkel Microscopy, Inc./Visuals Unlimited; **30 Corbis:** Visuals Unlimited (cla); **Corbis:** Frans Lanting (cr); **31 Corbis:** Adrianna Williams (c); **SPL:** BSIP VEM (cra); **Corbis:** Thomas Deerinck/Visuals Unlimited (fbl); **32 SPL:** Zephyr (cr); **33 SPL:** David McCarthy (tc); **SPL:** Eye Of Science (ca); **SPL:** Don W. Fawcett (c); **Corbis:** Visuals Unlimited (cb); **SPL:** Nancy Kedersha (crb); **SPL:** Steve Gschmeissner (br); **34 The Natural History Museum, London** (cl); **Corbis:** Tom Grill (bl); **35 Getty Images:** Allsport Concepts/Adam Pretty (tr); **Corbis:** Image Source (cr); **Getty Images:** Gorilla Creative Images/Lauri Rotko (br); **36–37 Getty Images:** The Image Bank/Urchin Rock – Professional Underwater Photography; **37 Corbis:** David Reed (tl); **Corbis:** Lester V. Bergman (bl); **Corbis:** Bob Krist (br); **38 Getty Images:** Steve Gschmeissner/SPL (tr); **Corbis:** Dennis Kunkel Microscopy, Inc./Visuals Unlimited (ca); **38 Getty Images:** Blue Jean Images (bl); **39 Getty Images:** Stone/A. Carmichael (bl); **Corbis:** Leland Bobbé (fbr); **Corbis:** Inspirestock (br); **40 Corbis:** MedicalRF.com (cla); **SPL:** Steve Gschmeissner (cra); **Corbis:** Photo Quest Ltd/Science Photo Library (bl); **SPL:** Susumu Nishinaga (br); **41 Corbis:** Philip James Corwin (crb); **Corbis:** Mika (br); **42 SPL:** Omikron (cl); **Getty Images:** Image Source (clb); **iStockphoto.com:** Johanna Goodyear (bl); **43 SPL:** Professor P. M. Motta/University "La Sapienza", Rome (tl); **Corbis:** MedicalRF.com (bl); **44 SPL:** Anatomical Travelogue (tc); **45 Corbis:** Jesus Diges/EPA (clb); **Corbis:** Peter Ginter/Science Faction (cr); **46–47 Corbis:** Dr. Richard Kessel & Dr. Randy K/Visuals Unlimited; **48 Corbis:** Dr. Fred Hossler/Visuals Unlimited (cra); **49 Corbis:** Dennis Kunkel Microscopy, Inc./Visuals Unlimited (clb); **Corbis:** Michael Haegele (br); **50 SPL:** Steve Gschmeissner (crb); **51 Corbis:** Ian Hooton/Science Photo Library (tr); **Corbis:** Klaus Rose/dpa (cr); **SPL:** Susumu Nishinaga (bc); **Corbis:** Radius Images (br); **52 Corbis:** Dr. Richard Kessel & Dr. Randy Kardon/Tissues & Organs/Visuals Unlimited (crb); **53 SPL:** Zephyr (cra); **54 Dorling Kindersley:** Onoky/Eric Audras/PunchStock (cla); **Corbis:** Biodisc/Visuals Unlimited (c); **SPL:** Professor P. M. Motta/University "La Sapienza", Rome (cr); **SPL:** Steve Gschmeissner (fcr, fbr); **SPL:** Biophoto Associates (bl); **SPL:** NIBSC (br); **55 SPL:** Science Vu/Visuals Unlimited (fcl); **Corbis:** Dennis Kunkel Microscopy, Inc./Visuals Unlimited (bl); **56 Corbis:** Veronika Burmeister/Visuals Unlimited (ca); **SPL:** Professor P. M. Motta/University "La Sapienza", Rome (c); **57 Corbis:** Image Source (ftl); **SPL:** BSIP/Cavallini James (crb); **58 SPL:** Roger Harris (tr); **SPL:** CNRI (bl, fbl); **59 Corbis:** Inspirestock (br); **60 SPL:** TissuePix (cb); **SPL:** Dr. Tony Brain (bl); **SPL:** Steve Gschmeissner (bc); **62 SPL:** Eye Of Science (clb); **63 Corbis:** Photo Quest Ltd/Science Photo Library (tr); **Science Photo Library:** David M. Martin, MD (cr); **Corbis:** Photo Quest Ltd/Science Photo Library (cra); **SPL:** Professors P. Motta & F. Carpino/University "La Sapienza", Rome (cb); **64 SPL:** David McCarthy (ca); **SPL:** Riccardo Cassiani-Ingoni (fclb); **Corbis:** Dennis Kunkel Microscopy, Inc./Visuals Unlimited (bl); **Corbis:** Visuals Unlimited (fbr); **SPL:** Steve Gschmeissner (br); **65 Corbis:** Dennis Kunkel Microscopy, Inc./Visuals Unlimited (cl); **SPL:** Professors P. Motta & F. Carpino/University "La Sapienza", Rome (cra); **66 SPL:** Alain Pol/ISM (br); **67 SPL:** Roger Harris (tr); **SPL:** Professor P. M. Motta/University "La Sapienza", Rome (bl, clb); **Corbis:** Ian Hooton/Science Photo Library (br).

Jacket images: Front: **Getty Images**: Digital Vision/Steven Errico (cb); Photographer's Choice/Thomas Collins (bc); **Science Photo Library**: Roger Harris (cl); Dr. Barry Slaven/Visuals Unlimited (c). Back: **Getty Images**: Photographer's Choice/Thomas Collins (cl); iStockphoto.com: Mischa Gossen (c).

All other images
© Dorling Kindersley
For further information see:
www.dkimages.com